The Loving Connection

A Love Story Between Heaven and Earth

D1603197

LeAnn Chen and Holly Lin

Contents

Part One

The Story of LeAnn
(aka Aesina)

Now, I am finally awake to the first ray of sunlight.
My every breath can start echoing the call of my true self.
It is time for me to gather the flowers from my garden of life.
It is time to present this bouquet to my family of the Universe.
It is time to testify to the loving connection between Heaven and Earth.

INTRODUCTION
The Budding Seed

I clearly recall the fright on my mother's face when I described certain events from the previous night. I had seen what she and others were doing and talking about, even though I was sound asleep at the time. I was about six years old. This information didn't just come to me in dreams. I saw things in the spirit realm that others couldn't see. People were often perplexed or awestruck when I told them about their lives or health conditions, despite having no prior connection with them. I often completed sentences for speakers because I knew what they were about to say. And I could describe events before they occurred, or that occurred somewhere far away without being present at the scene. I also had fun disclosing the gender of unborn babies for pregnant mothers. It shocked me the first few times when I perceived the impending death of people by looking at their faces. I was also able to connect with the spirits of the deceased. Often, I could understand the thoughts and feelings of animals, and I rescued a few of them in distress when the adults at the scene could not. I also enjoyed conversing with Mother Earth, hearing the stories of plants, and receiving their gifts of nurturing and healing.

My mom told me very early on never to talk about things of a non-earthly nature, such as ghosts or spirits. The reason she gave me was that I would scare and offend people. In my Asian community in Taiwan, people had worshipped gods at the temples for many centuries, and there were some spirit guides, fortunetellers, and witches. Apart from that, people did not feel comfortable encountering a supposedly normal person, especially an innocent child, who associated with spirits and the realm of the supernatural. They were fearful of the unknown—particularly the prospect of death. The general perception was that it was uneducated and superstitious to talk about spirits at that time.

I also had repeated vivid dreams of dancing and flying with ladies in beautiful, colorful chiffon dresses. These dreams began in my early childhood and continued into my mid-forties. Through the years, I also heard the fast whoosh of flying sounds next to my ears during sleep or shortly after waking up. The voice, or rather the thought, often impressed upon me in my mind's eye was, *You are an angel.*

Several psychics have told me that I emanate the vibration and energy of Quan Yin, the Goddess of Compassion. Numerous times while my physical body was asleep, but my mind was wide awake, I saw myself sitting on a rock in the shape of a lotus surrounded by a pillar of light. A team of handsome young men, grandly dressed in white uniforms, lined up on my left side. Beautiful young ladies in soft white dresses were lined up on the other side. The lotus I was seated on started to ascend inside the pillar of light wrapped around me and rose high into Heaven. The whole ritual unreeled like a film in front of me and the vision remains alive in me to this day.

Others have said not only that am I extremely compassionate but a powerful seer and reader as well. While giving me a reading, one psychic was surprised to discover that I was an angel of the highest rank, whose name translates to "The Nineth Heaven Goddess." Later, she would ask me to give her readings. A psychic master, who counsels many other psychics, once told me that I had a shining diamond on top of my head while giving me a psychic consultation. Sudden premonitions and inspirations also visit me in the form of visions, prompting feelings and visual and auditory impressions. This happens whether awake or asleep, and even while intently focused on tasks unrelated to the content of the visions.

I had never fully utilized these abilities, as I was busy trying to fulfill the demands of my everyday life. The concern about being judged negatively also weighed on my mind. I lead my life, with its ups and downs, like any ordinary woman. I am fascinated by biology, physics, chemistry, math, medicine, and health, as well as the research that connects discoveries in cosmology and physics with spirituality. Music, art, literature, dance, and nature can induce a state of bliss in me. I also enjoy reading stories about angels and testimonies of near-death experiences (NDEs), past life, reincarnation, and soul agreements. However, my personal beliefs about spiritual phenomena are primarily based on experiential evidence and that which can be proven with scientific instruments and supported by concrete research.

In 2007, the title of this book appeared to me one day like a big banner across the sky—*The Loving Connection*, and this urged me to start writing. As English is not my native language, my initial thought was: "Have I made a mistake? Why would '*ing*' be added to the end of 'love'? Isn't the word 'love' enough by itself?" I also had a few "why me?" moments and a sense of reluctance about this "extra responsibility" at a time when I was already trying to simplify my life. Having little experience as a writer, I also had doubts about my qualification to write a book. Since the core content of this book was not given to me in the initial vision, I thought that instead of searching for something new and unfamiliar to write about, it would be easier to talk about my own life experiences with a touch of mysticism for fun. Unexpectedly, working on my emotional shadows during the process of writing this book not only provided me much healing, but the closer connection with spirituality has also turned into a learning and growing journey for me.

Every individual has their own unique path in life. I enjoy exploring life and seeking truth like so many others. I don't lay claim to any "absolute" truths or pretend to have the final word on anything. I understand that wisdom continues to unfold, and there are always surprises in this mysterious Universe. What we perceive as true today may not be so tomorrow. The process of learning, experimenting, and evolving is never-ending. I continue to maintain a healthy skepticism in my investigations of spiritual realities and am excited about the information from everyone's discoveries.

I am deeply grateful to my wonderful family and friends, who have infused me with their love throughout this extraordinary time in my life. My wonderful friend Ina not only patiently listened to my stories with an open mind, but she also spent hours proofreading drafts of this story. Holly, my precious spiritual teammate, and the author of Part 2 of this book, was there from the start to offer her support in more ways than one. Our talented and beautiful editor, Kendra Langeteig, has made this book so much better than it otherwise could have been. Thanks to everyone's love and support, I was able to overcome my doubts about the visions and inspirations received from my Heavenly Parents, Archangel Michael, and other beings in the Heavenly realm, and step forward to share my story.

I hope this book will inspire you, dear readers, to explore the expression of love and wisdom in our mystical Universe. We all experience the intriguing, perplexing, and exhilarating moments of human life in our own unique ways. Let's support each other with compassion, respect, and gratitude along the way.

LeAnn Chen

I

The Dawn is Breaking

Invocation for Love

or years I had waited for my so-called soulmate to appear without having any luck. One day in early July 2007, I decided to test my "spiritual connection" by using a ritual from the book, *Archangels and Ascended Masters* by Doreen Virtue. Maybe my prince charming would jump right out of my insanely long wish list for the perfect mate! Nothing happened over the next few days after performing the invocation ritual suggested by the author. I felt a bit ridiculous and disillusioned, more so as the days went by. I was not born with the virtue of patience. So, I felt justified to pressure these invisible entities by giving them just one more day to show up or I would write them off. When I chanted the mantra one last time, I could not stop my silly grin at my clever threat. Surprisingly, a very strong and clear impression came and told me: *Instead of pleading with us, you should consult with Archangel Michael.*

What? So, they do exist? They can hear me! I gasped.

After conveying this message to me, these spiritual entities became still and silent. The energy around me became still as well. The hair on my arms was standing on end, and I had stopped breathing for a moment.

I was perplexed. "Why won't you help me?" I asked. "Aren't you supposed to be very compassionate and eager to assist us helpless earthlings?"

But no matter how much I begged and even tried to make them feel guilty, the entities were totally unresponsive to my pleas. Meanwhile, I could not fathom how I could understand them so well when just a minute ago I did not even believe in their existence. And who was this Archangel Michael anyway? So, I decided to consult Doreen Virtue's book once more.

She explained that it was up to us to personally invite the archangels to guide and assist us. Out of pure curiosity, and almost in jest, I closed my eyes and asked Archangel Michael to tell me about my soulmate. No sooner had my thoughts connected with his name than a feeling of love instantly infused my entire being. I had had numerous experiences with supercharged love and joy coming from entities in the spiritual realm. However, what I felt this time was different from my previous experiences; it felt strangely romantic.

As I was trying to figure out what this unusual feeling was about, I saw Archangel Michael open his beautiful wings and gently cradle me inside them. Naturally, I saw "wings" on him, since my earthly belief at that time was that angels had wings like in religious paintings and stories. It felt as if I was being buried deep in a soft and luxurious down cushion, caressed with the most exquisite tenderness. A distinct impression came to me: *He does not want me out of his arms. We have a very close relationship.*

The Spiritual Retreat

Betty is a very dear friend of mine who has the ability to communicate with spirits in other dimensions and cleanse houses from unwelcome spirits. Earlier that year, I had told Betty and Neal, another psychic friend, that I couldn't find my guardian angels even after trying the practices recommended by well-known psychics. Neal told me, "You will never find any guardian angels because you yourself are an angel!"

I was astonished by Neal's statement when I saw that he wasn't joking. Betty, too, was surprised. She decided to do a muscle test commonly used by spiritual workers to determine the truth of an event or a statement. When she held out her arm and asked, "Is LeAnn an angel?" the muscles of her arm did not contract. That meant, yes. This confirmed that Neal's observation about me was correct, but I remained skeptical.

Betty invited me to attend a spiritual retreat with her that July. I had never been to a spiritual retreat, and I was filled with curiosity and excitement about the event. While waiting to board the plane headed for the retreat, I told Betty how bewildered I felt about the idea of incarnated angels on earth. I shared the story of my brief experience with Archangel

Michael, which seemed too far-fetched to be real and had left me feeling exhausted. I asked her to explain what she knew about angels, since she had extensive knowledge about them. Then she paused for a moment, closed her eyes, and dropped into a state of deep reflection. When she opened her eyes again, she looked at me and said, "I think you are an archangel, it only makes sense."

To my utter amazement, as soon as Betty finished that statement, a tremendous surge of joy combined with immense relief gushed through my whole being. The uncertainty I had felt over the past few months about being an angel suddenly and completely vanished. It was like the brightest ray of sunshine piercing through thick dark clouds with a mighty force. The impact of this confirmation gave me a sudden burst of energy that I could barely contain. Not the least shadow of doubt could claim a place under such unequivocal assurance of my spiritual identity. No words could describe the exhilaration that ignited my being to the point of explosion. Betty and I were both in tears, succumbing to the powerful energy of the affirmation.

However, as amazing as this confirmation was, it could not prepare me for the unbelievable journey that I was about to undergo in the days and months to come. My critical and analytical abilities would be put to the test through the most crucial of challenges. And the flood gates between Heaven and Earth would be wide open to me from then on.

Discovering My Spiritual Name

I saw the word "Aesina" during one of the retreat sessions when I asked the Heavenly realm about my spiritual name. I had quickly dismissed that possibility, as I was still unsure about my ability to communicate with the spiritual realm. Nor could I really digest all this "angel business." However, on the morning of July 9th, as I was lying in bed, a very clear arrangement of the letters "A-E-S-I-N-A" was presented to me in my mind. I looked at this vision closely with my "spiritual eyes." And there it was, as clear as day: *AESINA*.

The Heavenly Parents (as I would soon discover) understood how I needed logical explanations and evidential support to be convinced about anything, especially when it came to mystical matters. So, they would offer me answers, usually when I was ready or when the timing was right, for a particular purpose. Their confirmations would come through coincidences, words, actions, people, media, sounds, light, feelings, and other unexpected occurrences. They would give me more visions or revelations, as needed, to help remove my doubts. Gradually, my mind and heart were able to comprehend things they would not otherwise be able to. Such was the case with my spiritual name, *Aesina*.

I did not realize the full implications of my spiritual name until a month after the retreat. On this particular day, my friend Holly (co-author of this book) asked me to give her an energy healing—a "spiritual administration," as I would later call the energy work that I perform with her. She arrived at my home at four o'clock that afternoon, still feeling weak from a recent illness, and we went into a quiet room to perform the healing session.

Holly felt totally energized afterward. She inquired about several spiritual terms that I could not explain, since I didn't understand their meanings either. Hoping to find some answers to Holly's questions, I reached for a book from the collection on my shelf: *Book of Angels* by Sylvia Browne, the well-known psychic. Although I had read the book years ago, I recalled little since I hadn't taken the ideas seriously at the time.

When I laid down the book on my desk, it fell open to a page where Sylvia Browne talked about a "Mother God." I still recall my surprise at coming across the mention of a female god. What I was familiar with was the male entity, omnipotent, omnipresent, and omniscient, referred to in almost every religion and by most people as the Heavenly Father, a male God. The male figure of Jesus Christ, the son of God, was revered almost as much as the Heavenly Father. Rarely had I heard or read a detailed discussion about a "Mother God."

I pointed to the heading on top of the page. It read: *"Archangels and Azra, the Mother God."* Somehow, I was prompted to look more closely at the spelling of Mother God's name. It was spelled "A-z-N-a," not "A-z-R-a," as I had first thought. This was not the first time my eyes had played tricks on me. I vaguely recalled previously mistaking an *R* for an *N* in the spelling of her name. Another inspiration made me say to Holly, "Mother God's name and my spiritual name both start with an 'A' and end with 'a.'" It later occurred to me that my mistakes concerning certain spiritual insights had been arranged for a purpose. However, neither Holly nor I took much notice of the observation I had just made.

When my spiritual name "Aesina" was revealed to me at the retreat, I didn't know how to pronounce it. I had placed the accent on *si*. But suddenly I was inspired to place the accent on the first letter, the *A* in Aesina's name. Curiously, I was also inspired to pronounce Mother God's name with the accent placed on the first letter—the *A* in "Azna." It was astonishing! Mother God's and my spiritual name sounded almost the same!

The realization shook me to my very core. My body felt like it was ready to explode from a massive electric shock. Hot tears surged from my eyes, and I choked while trying to contain my sobs: "Oh, my God! . . . Oh, my God!" Holly, who was sitting in front of me, watched me with her eyes wide open.

This incredulous information undermined my belief system and left me feeling a bit traumatized. I had to seek confirmation immediately. Instantly, the Heavenly Mother's golden light shot out brilliantly in front of me and was shining over my head. On my left side, I was flushed with the familiar bright white light from Michael. As my body was infused with this Heavenly energy, an announcement sounded mightily: *You were named after Mother God!*

My thoughts ran wild: *Me? Really? Why?* But then it occurred to me that the most important proof of my connection to Mother God was lacking. In my thoughts I asked myself: *If this were true, then why didn't I inherit the infinite power and wisdom of the Heavenly Mother? And why the different spellings?* I did not realize at the time that sounds and tones mattered more than spelling for spiritual names. In different languages, the spellings for a spiritual entity could be vastly different. Just as musical instruments are given different names in different languages, the instrument will produce similar sounds and tones regardless of its name.

More answers regarding spiritual names came a few days later when my earthly mother, who spoke Chinese and had learned a little self-taught English in her old age, asked me, "Why do these angels have names that are difficult for me to pronounce?"

Right after my mother's question, an illuminated cluster of symbols, much like a complex energy formula or a chemical equation, popped into my vision against the dark vastness of the Universe. This first symbolic form identified Michael. Soon afterward, different formulas for different archangels joined him, followed by trillions of other spirits. The formulas seemed to be moving faster than the speed of light. One after another they came, casting their bright forms against the blackness and filling up the mega screen of the Universe.

Each energy formula emitted a different vibrational frequency and a varied intensity of light. The whole Universe lit up brilliantly and joyously, as if everything had joined together in a celebration of life. It reminded me of snowflakes; each pattern is so unique, but together the lively snowflakes create a stunning whole. Like countless snowflakes, not even one of the spirits is exactly the same as any other.

For some unknown reason, I could understand what several Archangels were saying to me at the same time: *We have names that we prefer to be called on Earth. However, it really does not matter what names you call us. We know when you want to communicate with us and how to serve you.* Indeed, we can connect with spirits through the energy generated by our intention, thoughts, desires, or feelings.

Undeniably, names, titles, and rankings have a useful function in the human world. Nevertheless, the human ego often attaches values of superiority or inferiority to such labels. In the spiritual realm, each being is recognized by its individual vibrational energy and knows its own function to fulfill the purpose of the Universe. Each being is equally valuable, and unaffected by earthly names or titles.

The Unveiling of Aesina

Soon after I had received my Heavenly name at the spiritual retreat, a vision of Michael and Aesina as a couple came to me. Aesina was leaning affectionately against Michael's chest with the left side of her body. Michael held her right hand securely in his left hand, and he wrapped his right arm lovingly around her waist. He looked very handsome and powerful. An expression of joy, love, and contentment radiated from his face. A soft smile appeared and lingered as he looked at her with tenderness.

Aesina exuded serenity and sheer loveliness—an absolute exquisiteness and purity beyond words. Her entire body emanated an immense bright white light, tinted with the finest golden specks. I could not take my eyes off her. I was totally mesmerized by the most beautiful being I had ever witnessed in my entire life. *No wonder Michael is in love with her,* I thought. *Even I could fall in love with such magnificent beauty.* It was astonishing to consider that Aesina and I were somehow one and the same: *How could I be her, with my countless weaknesses and imperfections?*

The Crown

When Aesina appeared with Michael in my vision that day, I saw a gold crown around her head. I could only see the side view of the crown since the left side of her head was leaning against Michael's chest. The appearance of the crown puzzled me, but that did not impress me as much as the whole picture. I was fascinated and mesmerized by the immense beauty that Michael and Aesina presented together.

The next day, I got a full, front view of Aesina's crown. There was a large bright jewel in the middle of the crown. I was intrigued as to why a spirit body wore any adornment at all, especially a crown like that of earthly kings, queens, or people of high status. I still could not adjust my thoughts to the celestial frame. Our earthly world is, in fact, a minuscule replica of Heaven. Our imagination, creations, systems, and customs are often influenced by the memories of our life in Heaven.

An impression came to me: *The Heavenly Mother gave that crown to me when I was created.* The observation of the psychic that Betty and I had visited months before came into my mind, as he had seen a diamond shining on my head. Perhaps he had foreseen this jewel on Aesina's crown.

In my Heavenly vision, this crown somehow fit perfectly on my head, even as I grew from a baby into an adult. Looking back, I don't recall removing the crown on any occasion while living in Heaven. Perhaps that's because the crown was made of energy and could adapt to different shapes and sizes.

Another message came through from spirit, telling me that the jewel on the crown symbolized the third eye that helps people see the truth, and that guides them toward the light. As if to give me an illustration to help me understand the purpose of the jewel on Aesina's crown, an interesting vision followed directly on the heels of the message.

In this vision, I saw a ship on a tempestuous sea on a pitch-dark night. A lighthouse tower stood far away on a rocky cliff; its silhouette was visible against the treacherous sky. Aesina loomed over the lighthouse, looking gigantic compared with everything else in the surroundings. Similar to the lighthouse sending out its light, the jewel of her crown radiated extremely bright light. The skies were engulfed in the intense beam, while thousands of diamond-like flickers reflected upon the surface of the stormy sea. This representation seemed to say that our troubled souls shall find their way home by following the light.

Unexpectedly, Aesina's body started expanding outward until it filled every inch of space as far as the eye could see. Her looming figure became indistinct as she steadily blended in with everything around her. She was a part of and became One with the whole Universe.

The Struggle to Believe

I cannot adequately describe the extraordinary experiences that occurred nearly daily for over two and a half years, especially during those last several months in 2007 following the spiritual retreat. I had one intense vision after another, inspiration after inspiration, and sight after sight from the beyond. All of these visions, scenes, lights, and sounds from the spirit world were not only vivid in terms of their detail, but they were also forceful, and felt very real. They often occurred unexpectedly when my mind was engaged in simple everyday tasks, such as cleaning the house, and not consciously connecting to the spiritual realm.

As magnificent as these Heavenly encounters with Michael and my Heavenly Parents were, these visions inflicted tremendous torment, the likes of which I had never experienced. In my quest to discover the truth about Heaven and Earth, I struggled not just emotionally but also physically. I found myself constantly shifting between the earthly and spiritual realms, struggling to separate truth from falsehood, reality from illusion, while attempting to verify the existence of Heaven and its connection to Earth. My nervous system was often in a state of shock from the powerful impact of receiving this information from beyond the veil. My eyes were swollen from crying, and my heart burned in agony as I was torn between awe and disbelief, suffering from an inner conflict I could not resolve.

I was confused about my relationship with these angelic beings. Why was I allowed to associate with them in a way that most others on earth were not? It also seemed unbelievable that I could receive visions of what Archangel Michael and I looked like in our spirit forms and detailed scenes from our life together in Heaven. Many questions were eating away at me regarding Michael: Is Michael a "he"? Why do angels have genders? Why would there be an "us," an archangel and me, as a couple? Why does he, an angel, have feelings like humans— and more important, why does he have feelings for me?

For reasons I did not yet understand, despite my imperfections, I was allowed to witness the existence of the Heavenly Mother and the Heavenly Father. I saw how they conducted meetings and kept order in the Universe. Apart from enlightening me about how and why I was created, they let me witness how they created their spirit children. I also witnessed how they created material life forms and the stars. And I learned how they had nurtured and educated me from a little baby to adulthood. As Aesina, my spiritual being, I was Archangel Michael's beloved companion in the Heavenly home where I would receive his mentorship and love.

Amidst my miseries, I found solace by gently breathing the divine light into my being whenever my mind was confused and my heart felt troubled. In the tranquil stillness I was gradually able to appreciate the deeper meaning of it all with decreasing resistance and fear. I recognized that every existence is created out of the same source energy of the Universe with purpose, light, and love. We are all consciousness in form. Every one of our thoughts, deeds, and feelings postulates consciousness. The divine is in us, through us, and for us. It is not a misfortune or mistake but an honor and a privilege to hold the "golden ticket" to wear the earthly suit and cruise through this planet of dense emotions. Despite the division, conflict, disappointment, frustration, competition, chaos, disgust, or the apparent ugliness of it all, life is happening with us, through us, and serving us. Love is what life is, all that we are, and what truly matters. In the bosom of greater insight, I am empowered to receive love with less guilt and to express it with less fear. Consequently, compassion and gratitude have become my language of light. My heart is beautified by pure joy and perfect peace more often than before.

2

The Heavenly Mother and I

My Heavenly Mother's House

While I was going through my morning routine of self-healing and communicating with the Heavenly realm in March 2008, the Heavenly Mother appeared and showed me her house. I was surprised by this. *The Heavenly Mother has a house? Why do spirits need a place to live, especially when they are just energy? Why would Heavenly Parents live like earthly couples?*

Then I thought, *Maybe I have things backward again. Is this one more indication that the Earth is copying the Heavenly world?* I just could not wrap my head around it.

The home of the Heavenly Parents sits high above everything else in this realm. The palatial building is surrounded by tall white columns that rise from the ground to the roof, which is in the shape of a dome. It resembles the old temple of Athena in the city of Athens, Greece. There is a touch of intricate carving around the top of the columns. The majestic architecture is graceful and serene. Looking at it, I could feel a sense of simplicity, stability, strength, and timelessness in keeping with the character of the residents of this Heavenly house.

All spirits are equally loved by the Heavenly Parents and are allowed to create their own abodes to match their desires. Even though all are welcome, not everyone feels comfortable coming into the vicinity of Heavenly Parents' home. That is not because only important spiritual beings get invited but likely the choice of the spirits themselves. The force of light that emanates from the Heavenly home is too strong for most spirits to bear for long.

The Heavenly Mother and I walked through halls and rooms with extraordinarily high ceilings. The soft warm lights inside the house contrasted with the brilliant white light being emitted outside the building. The furnishings inside the Heavenly Parents' home were sparse and practical not decorative and lavish like in the homes of wealthy people on Earth, or in the gold-studded interiors of structures humans built to worship their gods. It was the finest example of living in a minimalistic way.

The Creation of Aesina

In my Heavenly home with Michael there was a spacious living room where my Heavenly Parents had created me. All the words on Earth could not adequately express my amazement at witnessing my spiritual birth in a vision received in August 2007. I saw the Heavenly Parents' arms extended and bent at the elbows, as if waiting to hold something together. After a moment of reverence and focusing their thoughts, a tiny baby appeared in their open arms. With much tenderness, they laid this sound asleep baby in an oval-shaped crystal crib. Archangel Michael, looking like an earthly seven-year-old boy, was also present. He was standing at the side staring intently, without so much as a blink. It was as if he was "holding his breath" during the whole process of this creation. This event was tremendously significant to him because the Heavenly Parents told him, "She is created for you as your Heavenly mate."

Baby Aesina had soft, short, silvery hair that flipped out at the ends just above her ears. Her bright dark eyes, shining like those of the Heavenly Mother, were set nicely on her perfectly round face. She was chubby all over, with short legs that made her wobble like a duck. She sucked her thumb all the time, whether she was asleep or awake. I could not help but think how adorable she looked.

My Heavenly Education

I saw myself as little Aesina, about the size of an earthly toddler, trying to keep up with the Heavenly Mother as she hurried along with her different tasks. Being so small, I could only grab the lower part of her long white dress. I sucked my thumb with the other hand while holding her skirt tightly.

(Interestingly, as a child on earth, I didn't stop sucking my thumb until well past the normal age for children, despite my parents' efforts to correct this "bad habit.")

The Heavenly Mother often took me along to different meetings and conferences that she and the Heavenly Father presided over. I would make a curtain to hide behind by pulling the lower section of my Heavenly Parents' robes together. Being very shy and not knowing what was going on, I wanted to shield myself from all those noisy adult spirits at the meetings. But curiosity often got the better of me, and my chubby little baby face would peek above this "security curtain." I saw my large round dark eyes survey around the room and look at everyone, wondering what they were discussing. Sometimes I saw my little body sleeping at the feet of the Heavenly Parents' feet after getting bored and tired. *Does the Spirit body need sleep?* I wondered when I saw this in my vision.

It was fascinating to learn that our spirit forms go through a process of growing and maturing from babyhood to adulthood, just like our bodies do on Earth. Our spirit body requires resting, nurturing, and strengthening just like an earthly body. The minds of our spirits also delight in continuously learning and expanding their knowledge.

Magic Candies

The Heavenly Mother showed me, through many visions, how she had trained and educated me as a child. At first, I couldn't help but think: *Why do I need an education? Don't angels know everything?* During one of my lessons in the Heavenly Mother's room, I could not help but be distracted by a basket that contained one of my favorite treats, candy-like fruits. I kept looking at the basket out of the corner of my eye; the fruits in various colors shone with a tempting light that lured my attention away from my lessons.

At last, the agonizing wait was over, and I was allowed to taste the fruits in the basket. I called them "the magic candies," as the Heavenly Mother and I could blow gigantic colorful bubbles in every shade imaginable with these chewy fruits. Afterward, we made music and all sorts of funny noises with these candies. The Heavenly Mother held my hands as we danced together, laughing and singing joyously.

Honoring the Sacred Mind

One morning, I saw the Heavenly Mother put me on her lap in front of something that I could not name. I smelled food, I heard birds chirping, I saw children crying . . . It was a hologram. I could see, hear, smell, touch, and feel everything that was shown to me. The Heavenly Mother asked me, "What do you see?" After I responded, she asked, "How does it feel?" Then she continued, "What would you like to do with this?"

I was impressed by the method of education that the Heavenly Mother had adopted. Rather than having Aesina learn about things from the theories or opinions of others in books, as children are taught to do on Earth, the Heavenly

Mother wanted me to learn to think critically on my own by having first-hand experiences.

No doubt the research and experience of our predecessors are valuable and should not be treated lightly. Nevertheless, it is vitally important to encourage children to learn how to think for themselves while expanding their knowledge. A child's mind is strengthened and grows through the practice of analysis and exploring questions, not by memorizing data and accepting the conclusions of others. Whatever we figure out through our own efforts will become a part of us and blossom into greater understanding and wisdom, while also shaping our character.

Field Trip

In another vision, I saw the Heavenly Mother taking me on a field trip on Earth. I looked to be around nine or ten years old, going by earthly age. We travelled through lands with rivers and mountains and visited various aspects of earthly life. We looked super-sized compared with the living things around us, and we were transparent as we stood there among them. I clutched my comfy toy tightly against my chest. (There were toys in Heaven, too. The toy was made of soft, velvety, colorful material that felt soothing to the touch, very huggable.)

I squeezed the Heavenly Mother's hand nervously whenever different objects, animals, and people moved through our transparent bodies, or weapons from battles flew through us. The Heavenly Mother stood patiently by my side while I watched intently everything that was happening around and through us. Such "real life" experiences were one of the methods that the Heavenly Mother used to broaden my observations, intensify my thinking, and strengthen my problem-solving skills.

From the Heavenly Mother's examples, I realized the importance of having an education from a young age that not only enriches the mind but also balances and harmonizes our heart, body, and soul. I also know that angels, who serve as nurturing assistants to the Heavenly Mother, watch over and guide our spirit as soon as we are created. This loving relationship between guardian angels and human spirits continues even after the spirit is fully grown. The angels, in essence, are extensions of our Heavenly Parents.

Angelic Works

In the Heavenly Mother's room, there was a very large and tall cabinet with complex carvings on its double doors. The Heavenly Mother led me to this armoire one day when I had matured to the age of an adult of about twenty-eight Earth years. When she opened the huge double doors, everything that had happened in the earthly world popped out right in front of me—past, present, and future, all at once.

It was like watching television shows livestreaming on multiple channels and screens at the same time. I saw wars raging in different parts of Earth throughout the centuries. I was shaken and pained to see the state of many countries in shambles, with destroyed civilizations, unending conflicts, darkness, and unrest. I witnessed people struggling in their mind, body, and soul. I heard cries of desperation and saw tears of immense sorrow on many faces.

There were brilliant rays of light scattering across the Earth and shining on rubble in different parts of the world at different times. Selfless deeds of courage, integrity, honor, kindness, and compassion rang with tonal harmonies accompanied by colorful lights. Thoughts and acts of unconditional love and gratitude generated the most powerful energy and the strongest light and music.

The Heavenly Mother then sent me to Earth attended by numerous other angels. We walked among the dead, the dying, the sick, and the tormented. Besides the awful stench, there were moans from the suffering. We comforted the wounded and attempted to ease their fear, misery, anger, and confusion by instilling hope in those who were willing to receive it. We held them in our arms and sent warm feelings of love into their hearts. We provided so-called miracles when help was needed at any time. No one is ever alone.

We were also busy helping those spirits whose earthly bodies were no longer useable or required to serve their purpose. We assisted these spirits back to our Heavenly home with words of encouragement, embraced them with unconditional love, and provided healing for their souls.

The Battle in Heaven

One morning in 2008, The Heavenly Mother showed me one of the most amazing visions I was given. I learned that to secure a peaceful life in Heaven requires vigilant safeguarding. The price we pay for freedom can be high, even in Heaven.

Instead of wearing the light-weight white dresses or robes that we usually wore, the Heavenly Mother wore a royal blue dress made of heavy, velvety material; I was dressed in a burgundy red dress of the same fabric. We were both wearing sandals instead of being barefoot as usual. The Heavenly Mother helped me put on armor and handed me a shield. She also handed me a scepter.

Why do we need this type of clothing? I wondered. The answer followed directly: *Because this gives you more protection from the dark spirits.* Then I asked, *With the shining jewel on my crown as the source of power and healing, why would I be holding a scepter in my right hand?* I had thought that the power of my thoughts alone was enough to carry out the mission. An answer came to me in response to this question: *It represents the source of power from Mother God.*

I then led a troop of warrior angels to a battlefield far away from the world where spirits live happily and securely. We were approaching a multitude of muddy gray, monstrous beings that had strayed from love and light. Light from the warrior angels and grayish sludge splashed all over the battleground as the angels fought these hideous beings. To my dismay and with an aching heart, I saw many warrior angels fall as the opposing force gained ground and became more and more difficult to hold back.

Suddenly, in a flash, the Heavenly Mother soared down to the battleground. As she swept over the field, light shot out of her eyes like sharp penetrating spears. The grayish creatures were destroyed, one after another, the instant they were struck by this powerful light. The remaining dark spirits snarled viciously, scrambled around blindly, and finally retreated. There were countless mounds of the vanquished left on the battlefield, grayish piles of the monstrous spirits and white piles of warrior angels.

The Mausoleum

With heavy hearts, the warrior angels and I gathered the lifeless forms of the deceased angels and took them back to our world of light. We approached a majestic white building in the shape of a dome, covered in a soft shimmering light. As we entered the dome, I saw a large concave altar in the middle of the room. A profound peace filled every space of this interior. I had never experienced such complete quiet and serenity. Reverently, we gave our thanks and paid respect to the deceased warrior angels as we laid their bodies at the altar. The energy of their life force, millions of sparks of light, had returned home to their Creator.

I realized that those gray beings had abused the precious free will endowed to us by our Heavenly Parents by choosing to disrupt the peace and order in Heaven for selfish gains. Our

Heavenly Mother (or Heavenly Father, who sometimes assigned Archangel Michael to lead his army of warrior angels to remove such threats) can remediate whatever fails to fulfill certain divine purposes. She had performed "the retraction of energy" from the gray beings and the fallen angels, whose forms were no longer functional due to the damage from the war.

Even though I knew that the energy of those departed spirits had merged with our Heavenly Mother, tears streamed down my face as I looked at the deceased warrior angels who were so beautiful and lively only moments ago. Strangely, I also had much compassion for those monstrous spirits in spite of their treacherous deeds. My heart could feel that the energy of the loving connection is what matters, not how we act or what we have become.

Life and Death

I was shaken to witness the "death" of a spirit. Without its light or unique energetic vibration, all that remains of a spirit is a gel-like substance. It reminded me how stunned I was when hearing the Heavenly Parents use the phrase "act of murder" during one of our communications not long before this battle. I had thought that energy could move or transform into a different design, character, or composition, even if its original host was no longer habitable. The way I thought of it, if there is no actual "death," then there can be no "murder" either.

Understandably, the sight of destruction, death, rage, and vengeance from the supposedly loving Heavenly Parents would seem like enough to turn people into atheists. How is it possible that love could be the force behind something that sickens us or breaks our heart? What makes the Heavenly Parents' seemingly atrocious deeds any less evil than the acts of cruelty coming from depraved human hearts? I discovered that the justification lies in the doer's intent and the kind of action executed.

Living in our dualistic and paradoxical earthly environment, humans tend to judge good or evil and right or wrong according to our conditioning—familial, educational, cultural, religious, environmental, and political. The circumstances, personal propensity, and free will of all those involved also contribute. We feel more comfortable when constrained by a predefined box that is understood and acceptable to our egoic mind. Depending solely on our limited and unevolved mind can stifle the intelligence of the heart and generate fear and insecurity due to irrational interpretations. Consequently, prejudice, biased judgment, hostility, self-sabotaging behavior, unkindness, and even destructive violence can arise in the attempt to eliminate these assumed threats. On the other hand, a purified mind can glue our heart and soul together and enables our divine love to purge away our ego and fear.

For the Heavenly Parents, murder seems to be equivalent to the despicable abuse of love. Nothing would exist without the energy of love, which is the source and substance of our existence. To remind us of our loving connection with one another, our Heavenly Parents made it obvious by having red-colored blood run through everyone's veins despite differences in race, skin color, or beliefs—as if to alert us that any intent or behavior contrary to love would be like draining the blood from a life; *an act of murder.*

Later, I also realized why the Heavenly Parents would retract energy and inflict "death" on their spirit children. During a spiritual administration with Holly in December 2012, the Heavenly Parents showed us how they created their spirit children. We learned that each spirit was given the free will to decide whether it wanted to be born, from the pure consciousness into a spiritual form. Every spirit is free to determine the particular characteristics it prefers, and it has the opportunity to preview its entire life, including the impact of the spirit's service during existence. Those deceased spirit beings at the battlefield, like all the Heavenly Parents' creations, already knew when and how they would cease to exist. They also had the choice to be recreated afresh according to their wishes. It is a fine example of co-creation between the Heavenly Parents and their spirit children. I believe the Heavenly Parents show the same beautiful respect and infinite love to all their other creations.

Without decay, calamity, and death, this Earth would implode from overpopulation. The chaos and violence resulting from the competition for resources, food, and living space would make it impossible for us to create a peaceful plant. The opportunity for innovations and the hope of "turning over a new leaf" on Earth would grind to a halt. Death and destruction are part of the divine plan of the Heavenly Parents.

Unlike humans, our Heavenly Parents are not plagued by negative feelings and emotions. Their intent is always to serve the highest good of all. They surely would not abuse their power or subject their beloved children or any of their other creations to any real harm, no matter the outward appearances. Death is the "New Life" in the hands of our Heavenly Parents.

The Birthday Party with My Archangels

Around the time of my birthday in July 2008, with my spiritual eyes, I saw the Heavenly Mother walking toward me. She said, "I want to take you to a party."

I was surprised but very happy. Anything to do with the Heavenly Mother made me feel extremely honored and thrilled. She encircled me with her left arm and took me to a room where I was greeted by a smiling Heavenly Father and all the other archangels. The thirteen archangels are like the high counsel members of the Heavenly Parents' parliament.

Instead of the simple white robes most spirits usually wear, every archangel on this day was dressed in very fine and colorful robes; their sleeves and necklines were fancily adorned, and they wore embellished belts. They were standing in front of me in a row, chatting joyfully. Michael came to stand by my side looking very happy and proud. *Why would he be proud of me?* I wondered.

All of a sudden, I saw someone on the left side of the front row. I could not help but run to him in excitement. *"Benny!"* I screamed. It was my eldest brother. We hugged tightly with much love and joy. Benny is in charge of caring for those spirits who suffer from trauma or become lost from the earthly experience. He would lovingly nurture and counsel them in a healing room that I called "Benny's Spa." Any spirit seeking realignment or rejuvenation of their energy, or in need of some TLC, is free to visit this spa any time.

A large, muscular gentleman in a tuxedo raised his golden goblet and wished me a happy earthly birthday. It was Archangel Chuck, the mightiest warrior in Heaven. He is our Heavenly Father's bodyguard and the gatekeeper between Heaven and Earth. He was usually clad in a masculine and "tribal" outfit to complete his menacing authoritative image. I was quite surprised to see him in such an elegant suit. I could not help but burst into laughter when he so uncharacteristically winked at me, imitating one of my favorite actors.

Then the nearly inseparable Heavenly mates Archangels Jake and Joleen greeted me. As usual, I was impressed by the exquisite beauty their appearance presented. They work as a team to inspire and stimulate the creative imagination of those in the spiritual and earthly realms. Extremely beautiful and powerful works of architecture, art, music, dance, literature, and performance are thus born and enjoyed by all. In the natural world, the formation of rocks and sands, the shifting of mountains and hills, the growth and decay of vegetation in forests—all of this is under their administration.

Walking toward me with a polished cane was the weather master Archangel Franklin, who oversees the changes, patterns, and effects of the climate on Earth. He likes to dress up and act like a British gentleman. Holly and I often laughed uncontrollably while imitating and teasing him about his accent. For revenge, one time while we were dining at a restaurant, he messed up our table setting to announce his presence. We had been talking about him at the time. Holly and I knew we should not interfere with his important tasks as weather master, but sometimes we asked him to bring us sunny weather for our outings.

As expected, standing next to Franklin was his buddy, Archangel Derek. Derek supervises the field of education. His demeanor is quiet, sophisticated, and scholarly. Besides developing and enhancing all aspects of knowledge, information, and learning skills, he makes sure these advancements are shared with all the beings in the Universe.

Archangel Eddie inched toward me and wished me good health. He works diligently not only to ensure the proper function of our spirit body, but also to inspire and assist humans with medical research for cures and health treatments. Since our minds are not limited by time and space, all medical and health information flows smoothly and unceasingly between dimensions for the well-being of our spiritual beings and earthly forms.

The gentle, lovely Archangel Diane came over and hugged me. We often connect with each other heart to heart. She observes and balances the effects generated by our complex human emotions and feelings. She inspires professionals and guides individuals on Earth how to preserve their mental and psychological well-being. We can find solace with the help of her unsurpassed knowledge, wisdom, and compassion.

A swish of joyful energy showered over me. I knew instantly it was Archangel John's doing. No one could manage energy as marvelously as he. John loves to regulate energetic currents with precision to ensure their speedy motion and transformations. He also has fun monitoring the creation, development, and operation of the transportation systems on Earth, as the energy that moves objects requires certain amounts of energetic power. He also recognizes that each thought, word, emotion, and action generate a specific energetic flow and entails proper maintenance to avoid malfunctions that could affect all there IS. He therefore diligently alerts humans to take heed of their thoughts, words, feelings, and deeds.

My eyes could not help but turn to a very solemn and authoritative figure who waited patiently to approach me—Archangel Marta. I have so much respect and reverence for her. She is the keeper of justice. The Laws of the Universe, including the law of cause and effect, are necessary to maintain order and avoid confusion among the trillions of spiritual beings that exist in the Universe. Justice on Earth often involves punishment, humiliation, material compensation, and the restriction of freedom. By contrast, Marta executes justice with supreme wisdom, guiding and healing with compassion, understanding, and immense love.

Raphael, the youngest archangel, skipped over to me with a mischievous smile on his face. He is like a busy bee, going around humans to administer his superior healing power over their physical suffering. Holly sees his emerald-green color nearly every day and has had much success utilizing the healing power of his light. Raphael's expression assured me that he still remembered our "faceoff"—I had complained jokingly to Holly that he had never shown me his "true colors."

It had happened one afternoon not long before this birthday party. Just as I was preparing to take a nap after an exhausting day, I saw something green flash past the corner of my left eye. Then a full view of Raphael suddenly popped into my sight. He was wearing a green ninja turtle headband, with a green-jeweled Elvis Presley shirt, a sequined scarf, and very tight glittering green pants flared with dark-green sequined insets. The green motorcycle he sat on was adorned with glittering green stones. *Green, Green, Green!* Nothing but green all over! Raphael could not have made his statement any clearer to me. He was displaying this lack-of-good-taste outfit on purpose. He looked ridiculous. I laughed so hard, my need for the powernap completely vanished.

As I was savoring the memory of Raphael's joke, a startling scene suddenly popped up in front of my eyes. I watched in disbelief as numerous little children streamed out among these big, tall archangels. They were of different races and were between the ages of two and seven. They were dressed in various styles suitable for different cultures. These children were getting ready to go to Earth.

Somehow, I could see *all at once* the kind of life each one of these children would be leading on Earth. I shuddered. These children would be despised, ignored, disrespected, disvalued, tortured, and starved. They would be lonely, poverty-stricken, disfigured, cheaply used, abused, humiliated, persecuted, and discriminated against. Many people on Earth would treat these tender souls callously, with contempt, disgust, and cruelty, just because they were different from themselves and were not deemed worthy of respect by their earthly judgment.

These children knew what was awaiting them on Earth. They were willing to use their presence to inspire compassion, equality, forgiveness, medical and health advancements—and most important of all, love, in the human world. They felt honored and were committed to their mission on Earth. They looked forward to the experience of their own spiritual evolution as they aspired to encourage the expression of the beautiful essence in others.

I felt so much respect and compassion for them that I could not help but drop down on my knees to gather all of them in my arms. Yes, *all* of them. Somehow the magic of energy enabled my arms and body to easily expand to accommodate them. I saw tears pouring down the face of my spiritual body and from my earthly eyes, too.

I was stunned and touched beyond words by their courage and respected their decisions. Yet my heart was filled with indescribable pain at seeing the sufferings they would be going through. Looking at each one of their beautiful and contented faces, I was humbled and felt embarrassed that I had moaned and complained about my earthly challenges. These children are my finest examples, my teachers, and my role models.

Why bring out these children at my birthday party? I wondered. *Am I supposed to repent for my ignorance and ingratitude upon seeing how much more courageous these children are than me?* I was deeply ashamed of my countless weaknesses.

Reading my thoughts, a distinct soft voice came to me: *It is the other way around.* I had always been uneasy about taking credit for anything, so I ignored this small voice and continued suffering in shame. But the Heavenly Mother could not stand to see how expertly I was torturing myself. There was a hint of laughter in her voice as she approached me and said, "Why do you think we got together to celebrate your special earthly day? Why did Michael look so happy and proud? We are proud of you because you have made it thus far on Earth. We wanted to assure these children that they can make it too. You are a fine example for them as we are aware that while earthly experiences are most effective in speeding soulful evolvement and energetic expansion for the Source, they are very challenging nevertheless."

She continued, "We promise to always protect and support you and every one of these children. We will be there for all of you every step of the way. Don't be afraid. We love you!"

The Gift of Free Will

One morning, soon after I'd sat down quietly to connect with the spirit world, a vision appeared. I saw Michael standing at his usual spot at the front left side of the living room in our Heavenly home. The Heavenly Mother was standing on the right side as usual, while the Heavenly Father was standing just a few steps behind her. Their placement often formed a triangular shape.

I asked Michael and my Heavenly Parents why they had let me go down to Earth, knowing all the pain and hardship I would have to face. *Wouldn't Michael miss me?* I thought. Despite showing his pride in me, my heart sometimes felt his sadness of missing me when I connected with him.

Michael said, "You wanted it."

I thought he must be joking. I turned to the Heavenly Mother in disbelief, hoping for a different answer. "You wanted it," she confirmed.

Feeling even more frustrated, I turned to the Heavenly Father, hoping for a more agreeable answer, since he had always shown me more indulgence.

He said solemnly, "You wanted it."

Three strikes!

I was sure they were either terribly wrong or just teasing me. How could three of my most trusted and beloved family members treat me like that?

I don't believe you! Why would I be so stupid to want such a challenging life? I screamed in my thoughts at them.

"Haven't you enjoyed some fun on Earth?" They asked.

"Yes, but..." I rejected their reminder, even though I knew what they said was true.

Not only was I filled with doubt and anger, but I also felt extremely resentful. Why would I subject myself to prejudice, discrimination, humiliation, and injustice? Why would I want to live in constant fear, shame, guilt, regret, and make embarrassing mistakes? Given a choice, I would not be so foolish as to be part of a world raging with cruel wars, natural disasters, and human treachery. It was unlikely that I would desire a life of misery and never feeling I was good enough. I would certainly not ask for an imperfect physical body with limited mobility and constant aches and pains. And I believed that I would be sensible enough not to get involved with the formidable ego on Earth. All that I could see at that moment were the negative aspects of my earthly life.

Something white suddenly sprang up right in front of me. I caught it instinctively with both hands. "Fur Ball!" I exclaimed. It was one of my favorite Heavenly pets: soft, round, furry, and white. All my pets came over and surrounded me. The small ones were squeezing and crushing against each other at my feet, trying to get near me, while the larger ones gathered around us. I recognized a couple of the huge, strong ones towering over me. I remembered the occasions when these huge creatures had flown me to places, such as the battleground with the other angels. I called out the name of each of my pets with great delight. Soon, I was lying on the floor and rolling around with them. The air was filled with my giggles and their squeals.

My innocent pets were obviously pure in heart. They were neither affected by nor seemed to care how serious my confrontation with Michael and the Heavenly Parents had been for me. They simply made their presence known with this show of love and support.

Suddenly I felt very angry again and thought: *There is no way I would leave my adorable pets, my beloved Heavenly mate, my beautiful Heavenly home, and the perfect life in Heaven with my Heavenly Parents.*

"I want to be 'home' now!" I demanded.

Sensing my sorrow and indignation, the Heavenly Mother said, "You can always come home, anytime."

"Really, but how? Mustn't I die physically on Earth first?" I asked. But I received no answer. It was much later before I would understand that our spirits can go back to their Heavenly home whenever they desire, whether through our thoughts, during meditation, or while asleep. We are home when the state of our mind is in clarity and stillness, our heart sings the beauty of gratitude and loving Oneness, and our being resonates with the vibrational frequency of the divine consciousness.

The Heavenly Library

While filled with resentment over the next few days, a vision of myself as a teenager in the spirit world came to me. Tears were streaming down my sorrowful young face as I watched the extent of suffering humans were going through on the Earth. I was confused and devastated, feeling so sad for my dear earthly brothers and sisters. The Heavenly Mother, who was sitting next to me, counseled me with great patience and gentleness. However, I could not understand the reason for all this suffering, nor was I persuaded by her explanations.

In my heart, I protested: *Why is it necessary to go through such severe challenges to achieve spiritual evolvement and fulfill a higher purpose for the greatest good? What is the greatest good anyway? And for whom?*

I went to the library to do further research on this issue. Yes, there is a place in the spirit world where massive volumes of information are kept. A few years after this vision, I learned they are called "The Akashic Records" on Earth. After studying intensively, and carefully examining cases of human existence throughout time, I decided that the best plan was for me to experience earthly life in person. Perhaps I wanted to verify things personally rather than believe what my Heavenly Parents had told me. I noticed that I demonstrated a similar curiosity and determination in both the spirit and the earthly realms.

Months later, after many more experiences through my visits to my Heavenly home, I further affirmed that the reason I came down to Earth was to satisfy my inquisitive mind. I was someone who needed proof and evidence to support the truth about questions that I had. Michael and the Heavenly Parents respected my free will and did not object to my choices no matter what they felt about it. They knew that even if they had tried, they would not have been able to stop me.

Favorites

One day when sitting together in the garden, the Heavenly Mother surprised me by saying, "You are our favorite child."

I instantly felt troubled and distressed. *How can Heavenly Parents have favorites? Don't they love each one of us equally? Maybe they say that to every one of their children?* I thought I must have heard her wrong.

Seeing my painful exasperation, the Heavenly Mother asked me, "Do you like flowers?"

"Yes, I do. They are so beautiful," I said, looking at the profusion of flowers in the garden.

"Do you love all flowers even though they have different colors, shapes, sizes, and fragrances?" she continued.

"Yes, I love them all and cherish ALL of them," I emphasized.

"Do you have any favorite flowers?"

"Yes. The long-stem white roses."

Having made her point, she did not go on any further.

Much later, I would realize that since all of us are created with different attributes, we thus have our own preferences and favorites. Naturally, not everyone's preference will be the same. How liberating it is to know that we are encouraged to be our authentic self! We can enjoy our preferences without attaching to them, value our emotions without getting stuck in them. This divine arrangement empowers our creativity and enriches the world.

Coming Home

The Heavenly Mother and I would often walk hand in hand to a lovely green pasture that stretched far beyond sight. She would sit down against an ancient tree, and I would lay my head on her lap. She would kiss the jewel on my crown, and then look at me with a very tender expression on her face. I melted completely as I beheld the purest and most perfect Heavenly beauty in front of me.

Sometimes she would brush away a few strands of my hair from my face while singing to me. I would become calm and relaxed and feel invigorated and courageous once again. I felt safe from whatever was troubling me in my earthly experience. I was so at peace that I could have purred like a little kitten in the arms of her adoring master.

Cradled inside the Heavenly Mother's loving presence, I felt that I had truly come home. I sighed with great contentment as tears streamed down from my eyes. I couldn't help but say, over and over again, "Mother, I love you so much . . ."

3

The Heavenly Father and I

uring my childhood, I had no idea what the Heavenly Father was like or whether such an entity truly existed. I did not think much about it, since I lived in an Asian culture that was a mixture of predominantly Taoism, Confucianism, and Buddhism. The limited concept I had of a fatherly "God" came from pictures and stories I had come across while growing up. Later I attended a church in Taiwan and learned about the Father, Son, and Holy Ghost from the Bible. Eventually, I was baptized at this church, where I met and married my first husband, and with whom I would have my two children.

The Heavenly Father that I had seen in numerous visions in 2007 had short hair with a silver hue like that of the Heavenly Mother's. I remember the Heavenly Father's smile and chuckles, as well as his silvery eyes that emitted brilliant light shining with love, wisdom, and humor. He was gentle and easygoing but carried himself with an air of authority and power.

I will always savor the memory of me as little "Aesina" sitting on his lap. My eyes still get misty when I think about his arms wrapped around me so protectively and lovingly. He also would let me swing like a monkey on his strong arms and hop and skip around his feet. His smile reflected in his eyes whenever he looked at me, sometimes with a bit of mischief in them too. He laughed merrily at whatever I said, and even when I messed up his silvery mustache. Oh, how I miss those chuckles!

He took me many places to educate and cultivate my soul. I was amazed to see that we could even walk on the oceans and rivers. I did not realize until much later that since we are all made of energy, this means that it is possible to work with energy and make adjustments appropriate to our circumstances. I also remember how puzzled and confused I felt when I saw myself as a toddler sitting on the Heavenly Father's lap and clapping my hands with joy after listening to me as an adult perform a song at a recital. How could I be the child and the adult at the same time? I had no understanding then of the concepts of simultaneity and parallel universes.

Heavenly Creation of the Earth

In early March 2009, while sitting on a bench enjoying the peaceful ocean view, an unexpected vision appeared when I closed my eyes. I saw myself as a little child of about five or six years old, standing next to the Heavenly Father. He pointed out certain scenes in the spirit world to me, and then showed me scenes on Earth that appeared to be just like those in Heaven. He explained that the purpose of this resemblance was to ease the shock and help us to adjust to life on Earth as we lived through our physical experiences there.

An intense scene followed. The Earth was filled with flowing hot liquid; orange mixed with different shades of red. I realized that the flowing liquid was lava, after which I saw a scene with volcanic formations. The orange-red lava flowed into volcanic rocks and formed mountains and hills. As the scene continued, the Heavenly Father never let go of my little hand, probably knowing that I would be intimidated by the massive construction.

A vast ocean appeared in front of us soon after, winding around the mountains and circling the earth. I saw gigantic whales swimming in the ocean. As I began to wonder about the smaller fishes, I saw the Heavenly Father extend his right arm and throw something into the ocean. Just then, thousands and thousands of sea creatures of all varieties instantly appeared. The Heavenly Father made the same throwing gesture once again. Millions of living things, so many I could not even begin to name them, appeared in front of us. They took on their individual roles, while also being connected to each other in the great cycle of life. I watched them roam around the majestic mountains, run through the rolling hills, and fly over the enchanting forests. Some of them strolled along the winding rivers; others grazed in the tranquil green pastures or hopped among the bushes. There were countless creatures busy with various roles under the ground, too.

Next, the Heavenly Father squatted down beside me and drew something in the sand. I don't recall much of what he said, but I knew that it was about some plans. What I do remember clearly are these words: "I am showing you the Creation of the Earth!!"

I did not realize that the Heavenly Father was using energy to create those life forms, until I later witnessed how he and the Heavenly Mother used energy to create their spirit children and other beings—material earthly incarnations and non-material beings such as our galactic star families. They directed and managed everything that exists in the Universe with energy. It also took me quite some time to learn the significance of my relationship with the Heavenly Father's creations on Earth. I realized that all living beings—from rocks, plants, animals, and water to Mother Earth herself, as well as the systems and programs developed to sustain our life—are manifested through God's loving and intelligent plan to support us for the greatest good.

The School of Life

Once the stage has been set and we are born into a physical body and start to grow up, an "ego" joins our true self on the earthly journey. In contrast to the Oneness we knew in the spiritual realm, we now have to experience competition, comparison, separation, oppression, hypocrisy, lies, and persecution on Earth. We also must have experiences in which fear and feelings of unworthiness, or lack (not being good enough), overpower our feelings of security, wholeness, and abundance. No longer an eternal body in its strongest and most perfect state, our mortal form is susceptible to diseases, aches and pains, aging, and death. We often find ourselves trapped in shame, guilt, regret, remorse, jealousy, frustration, and the sorrow of rejection rather than enjoying the harmony and bliss we once knew. Judgmental attitudes of prejudice and discrimination inhibit our appreciation for the rich diversity of differences. Of course, light can shine through the dark clouds when our mind, heart, soul, and spirit restore their equilibrium with divinity once again.

Wherever I go in life, I always meet many loving and kind people. Yet I have also endured the humiliating experience of being treated with disrespect, like a lowly animal, and I have faced phony politeness and bigotry more often than I care to mention. There were times when my kind deeds, hard work, honesty, and integrity were not valued over my gender, race, or financial and social status.

I remember an encounter with discrimination soon after my then-husband and I had moved to Dallas, Texas. One day while shopping at a grocery store not far from our home, I noticed a man following me closely down every aisle in the store. It was unsettling, and I couldn't understand why he was doing it. Finally, I politely asked, "Is there anything I can do for you?" He identified himself as the hired security for the store and told me bluntly, "I am making sure that you are not shoplifting." He continued to trail me until I walked out of the store, after paying for my groceries. This memory haunted me for years.

In the Shadows

While writing this chapter and connecting with the Heavenly Father, many painfully dark scenes from my first marriage flashed vividly before my eyes, one after another.

A sharp pain pierces my heart when I recall finding my four-year-old son sitting on the front steps of our home. He looked at me with a sad and lonely expression; a pair of his tiny shoes were placed neatly next to him. When I asked him what he was doing, he pointed his little finger to the door and said, "I want to go away, Mommy. I want to go away." *So, he senses the cold and loveless situation we are in at this home,* I realized. With tears streaming down my face, I wrapped my little boy in my arms and carried him away from the door. My heart bled with anguish for failing to protect my son and give him a happy home. To this day, I can still taste that excruciating pain.

Another scene from our life in Saudi Arabia rolled in. One rainy night, my then-husband was driving so recklessly that my son and daughter were thrown around in the back seat. When I asked him to slow down, he screamed at me to get out of the car and left me on the side of the road, miles from our house. There was no public transportation in that area, and I had no money with me. I was immediately drenched by the cold rain. At that moment, I didn't care if I found my way back home, since I did not feel there was a "home" for me to return to. Overwhelmed by sorrow, I didn't care about my safety either, even though I had heard many stories about women being raped or killed in a country where a woman's worth was valued by the number of the sheep she brought to the marriage.

Somehow, I was able to reach home by late that evening. The house was quiet when I walked in, as my family was asleep. I was greeted by an open empty suitcase on the floor inside the front door. As soon as my then-husband got up the next morning, he pointed to the suitcase and ordered me to leave with my son because my son and I "turned him off." I remembered his embarrassment when his colleagues commented that my son did not look like him. He was an American, a Caucasian, and my son looked more Asian—more like me.

The Lure of Addiction

My then-husband's frequent verbal abuse made me feel as if my life was worth less than dirt to him, that I was an annoyance. He insulted me by saying that I had come from the gutter; that I looked funny and smelled foul. He reminded me not to talk too much as my English was flawed, my tone sounded harsh, and my accent was irritating. He said that those who praised my good looks or appreciated my talents were just being nice. Using his mother as a comparison, he pointed out how horrible a mother I was. Worst of all, he attributed his pornography addiction to my imperfections as a woman and wife.

I remember his mother telling me in the first year of our marriage that she had found my then-husband's pornography collection before we were married. Our marriage counselor informed me that addictions such as his usually started as a teenager. Even so, my shame and guilt for being a failed wife and mother would devalue me for decades.

Not long after our wedding, my then-husband and I drove into the city. After checking out the adult entertainment district, he left me on the corner of a downtown street nearby and told me to wait there. He didn't say where he was going or when he would return. I didn't dare to move away from that corner for fear of getting lost or missing him when he came back. I soon started to feel very uncomfortable because a policeman kept inspecting me from head to toe. My face turned red when I realized that I was standing on a corner where prostitution was conducted. Although I had to suffer through another hour of shame before my then-husband picked me up, I did not voice any complaints, since I felt I had to be the submissive, obedient wife.

Several years later, a similar thing happened while traveling through a city with our small son. My then-husband scouted the district for adult entertainment, then he dropped off me and our toddler in front of a small hotel and told me to wait there. It was a chilly and gloomy day. To shield us from the harsh weather, I took my son in his stroller inside the hotel lobby. We squeezed into a corner of the tiny lobby so as not to interfere with the hotel patrons. Our helpless plight elicited sympathy from the hotel clerks, who allowed us to remain in the lobby. Not only were we hungry and cold but my legs felt numb from standing there for hours by the time my then-husband returned. But being the obedient and subservient wife, I voiced no complaints when he showed up without any explanation or words of concern.

***

Next, this incident surfaced in my mind. My then-husband's cousins, who lived near us in Saudi Arabia, had invited us to join them at a popular market. They had forewarned us that women needed to be protected from the sexual advances of the male patrons in the crowded marketplace. When we reached the market, my then-husband's cousins wrapped their arms around their wives to protect them. Whereas my then-husband immediately disappeared into the crowd. I pushed my one-year-old daughter in a stroller with one hand, while holding onto my five-year-old son's hand with the other, as I squeezed through the jam-packed crowd of men to find my then-husband. Suddenly, someone grabbed my buttocks. Instinctively, I slapped the man on his bony back and shouted angrily at him, which turned many heads. The men around me burst into laughter. My heart pounded from shock, shame, and embarrassment as I rushed to find my then-husband and relate the incident to him. I could not believe my ears when he said to me with disgust, "How could you do that? Don't you know he hasn't had any women for a long time?"

All sorts of awful emotions surged through me long after that experience. Not only did I feel victimized, violated, and incensed, I also could not wash off the nauseating feeling of shame and uncleanliness.

Path to Freedom

I remember locking myself in the bathroom and sobbing helplessly: "My children! My children! . . ." I didn't want to upset my little ones by crying in front of them. They were the reason I chose to stay in this unhappy marriage to their father for as long as I did. Eventually, I went to my only safe harbor by flying with my children from Saudi Arabia to Taiwan, where my loving parents lived. Out of sheer will power, I managed the connecting flights with a toddler, a baby, a heavy stroller, two pieces of luggage, and carry-on bags. Reaching my parents' home, my heart was full of pain for bringing this shame upon them and making them so sad and worried.

One morning, while dressing my small son, I was thinking about getting a divorce. It was a terribly scary prospect, especially since I didn't know anything about the legal rights that protected women financially in a divorce. How would I support my children? I certainly would not want to burden my elderly parents. My heart ached with pain. Many women whom I knew personally were struggling to feed their children after getting a divorce. I feared that I would deprive my son and daughter of a comfortable life if I chose divorce. I still remember the power of the love for my children piercing through my being which sealed my determination to return to my then-husband. So, I flew back to my then-husband with my two little children. But within a week, I knew I had made a terrible mistake that would trap me in tremendous sorrow for years to come.

After a failed attempt at marriage counseling, I proceeded to file for divorce. I doubt that I would have had the courage to pursue the divorce had I foreseen the corrupt and long-drawn-out divorce proceedings ahead. My eyes were opened for the first time to the extent of the cruelty and deceit that human beings were capable of. I was sickened to see how my then-husband used my children as pawns in the divorce court to protect his reputation and for his financial gain. Many times, I pleaded with my then-husband to settle our finances fairly to avoid legal costs, but to no avail.

My then-husband and his attorney characterized me as lazy and dependent for not working outside the home. In truth, I was following the teachings of our church to be a full-time mother and wife, and our finances were in good order. They also painted me as an irresponsible, immoral, selfish woman who was heartlessly abandoning her children by filing for divorce. When asked about my plans to secure a livelihood, I said that I wanted to pursue a career in the medical field. For as long as I can remember, I had desired to heal people. They laughed in my face and accused me of being a money-grabber and branded me as a "professional student."

Besides framing me as worthless and immoral, they dragged my parents into their despicable scheme. To go after my parents' meager life savings, my then-husband and his attorney concocted a story that tarnished my parents' noble characters and good name. They urged the court to deport my parents for a dishonest deed that had in fact been committed by my then-husband. I discovered from this experience that to see my loved ones suffer because of me was the utmost anguish in life.

In God's Hands

After two years of this legal battle with my then-husband, all the while worrying about the financial drain, I was exhausted emotionally, mentally, and physically. One evening while sitting on my bed and talking with my parents in Hawaii to update them on the situation with the court trial, I broke down and wept like a lost child. To hear my parents' voices filled with sorrow and worry felt like thousands of knives slicing through my heart. I truly wished that I would not wake up the next morning, as I had already died a thousand deaths from a broken heart and despair.

As soon as I hung up the phone, a vision appeared. I was inside a sphere with billions of extremely tiny particles hustling and bustling around me. A gigantic hand appeared that seemed to fill up the whole space with its sheer size. It picked me up from the frenzied and chaotic mess of a life I was in and placed me in a world that was devoid of anything—no sound, no activity, nothing but exceedingly bright white light. Somehow, I knew that it was the Heavenly Father's hand that had picked me up and placed me in that Nothingness. A soothing sensation entered the tips of my toes and flowed up my entire body to the top of my head. Without my own volition, the smooth motion of energy gently pushed me backward against the bed, and I was sound asleep before my head even touched the pillow.

My worried parents did not sleep that night, but waited to call me at 6:30 a.m., my normal waking time, the next morning; it was 3:30 a.m. in Hawaii. They wanted to offer me their comfort and support. I told them about the incident that had occurred the previous night. I told them that not only had I slept through the night (which rarely happened), I also felt remarkably refreshed. I was very happy and felt like giggling for the first time since the divorce proceedings had begun. I could hear the relief wash over my parents. They encouraged me to remember this as a sign and continue to do what was right.

Divine Justice

For a few years, I had been attending temple sessions on Saturday mornings. An amazing revelation took place one Saturday morning in 1999, just weeks after I had asked God to show me his justice. During the session at the temple, a scene with a woman imploring God kept popping into my mind's eye. I thought it was from a picture I had just seen in which

Mary was kneeling in front of Jesus being resurrected from his tomb. I tried to brush the scene from my mind, and I was bewildered to see that it persisted.

The final part of the session that day was held in a magnificent room known as the Celestial Room. In the mornings, it was usually filled with a soft light that filtered through the floor-to-ceiling windows on the east side. Strangely, on this particular morning, the room was flooded with an immensely intense white light that nearly blinded my eyes. I looked for my longtime friend Trudy, who usually accompanied me at the Saturday morning sessions. By squinting my eyes, I was barely able to detect a vague image of her sitting on a sofa on the opposite side of the room. I walked carefully toward her to avoid tripping, since the bright light made it difficult to distinguish the objects in the room.

I wondered where all the other patrons had gone. On Saturdays, the temple was usually filled with a large crowd of attendants, including local people and others from nearby cities. Somehow, even the on-site matrons had disappeared. Trudy and I were the only ones in this huge room.

"Isn't it bright this morning?" I said, when I finally reached Trudy.

"Yeah, so bright . . ." she replied.

I sat on the sofa next to her and attempted to enjoy the aesthetic beauty and serenity of the room, as I usually did. However, the light had wiped out any discernable features of the furniture, walls, windows, and decorations in the room. Moments later, the same vision I had seen earlier popped up again. Only this time, it was like watching a movie on a gigantic high-definition screen with a 360-degree view. The Heavenly Father was standing there in his white robe listening to me, while I sat on the floor in front of him pleading for justice for myself and all women.

Within what seemed like only milliseconds, I saw my ex-husband, also in a white robe, kneeling in front of the Heavenly Father. He was holding his hands together and his arms were extended upward towards where I was standing on the left side of the Heavenly Father. Words entered my being: *He is begging for mercy!* The remorse that my ex-husband was feeling was terribly painful and I immediately felt a surge of compassion for him.

The powerful impact of this vision shook me to my core. Trudy was very concerned when I began sobbing. Choking from the tears, I said, "I saw my ex-husband begging for mercy in front of the Heavenly Father."

After this incident at the temple, every part of me felt strange. An unaccustomedly strong energy permeated every space inside and outside of me. Gentle white light, soft and sweet like cotton candy, wrapped my entire body for two weeks afterward. A message impressed upon me during all that time: *Be not lost to the world.*

This vision of the Heavenly Father and myself in the temple seemed to be a sacred design to satisfy my notion of what justice should be according to the level of my understanding at that time. It helped to release my indignation about the many facets of inequality on Earth, especially regarding gender and race. In addition, it enabled me to understand what the Heavenly Father meant when he told me at the temple, "God's justice is different from men's justice. Each one of you is your own judge."

Not understanding God's justice, I had thought it meant to uphold the applicable laws and regulations with equity, which usually involves various types of corporal punishment, limitation of freedom, or financial restitution. I now realized that God's justice is synonymous with the "Service of Love": to reconcile, educate, guide, and heal. To put it another way, God's justice is the gift of Divine Grace.

I also saw that the reason we are supposed to "be our own judge" is because our true self is the light of pure consciousness—which is all-knowing, with perfect intelligence and unconditional love. Our true self can clarify right from wrong and offer appropriate remedial solutions. Also, in divine light, gratitude replaces the feelings of being wronged, which will then render the process of forgiveness redundant. That is because our true self can appreciate that our perpetrators may have been our beloved spirit brothers and sisters who have agreed to collaborate with our curriculum to fulfill the intention of our soul or to balance our karma.

Another purpose for God's justice is to preserve, protect, and honor the ethical codes in life. We are asked to stand up, speak up, and clean up all that is contrary to love. We can help to implement a better moral practice for all, with ready skills, fine examples, and informed advocacy. Moreover, when called upon to educate, counsel, or choose remedial measures to defend the well-being of all, we must execute the principles and rules that endorse love, equality, integrity, and the sharing of abundance without discrimination, prejudice, favoritism, self-interest, or greed. Of course, it is preferable for all actions to be done in a peaceful, non-destructive manner.

Indeed, God's justice is not designed to punish, humiliate, or decrease our value or worthiness. Its purpose is to lead the spirit involved and those concerned to the divine truth and heal them with His infinite love. Ultimately, to live the truth of God's Justice is to see God in everyone and everything, and be the grace of God to honor all in loving Oneness!

Compassion and Wisdom

Through this Heavenly insight, I realized that even though every spirit is designed to continue learning and evolving through its earthly experiences for the greatest good of all, some spirits could get lost in the earthly role they take on. Every earthly experience gives us the choice whether to endorse ego, or be the expression of love and create beauty.

Empowered by the love and compassion inherent in our souls, I was able to see there was a frightened little boy in my ex-husband, who was overwhelmed by the challenges of the unceasing demands of life; the heavy responsibilities involved in marriage, family, and job. There was a scared little girl inside me, too, who was lost in it all. I came to see that in relationships, not only are we there to offer each other safety and loving companionship, we are also each other's practicing ground for learning and spiritual growth. We are like a surgical knife that's used to dissect each other's pain body to reveal unhealthy anomalies, to repair, heal, and perfect the desired advancement of our soul with understanding, forgiveness, patience, wisdom, and love.

Feeling my ex-husband's immense sorrow in that vision led me to realize as well why we would feel thousands of times more intensely in our spirit form the consequences of our earthly thoughts and behaviors. It is because in the state of pure consciousness, our spirit can experience empathy and compassion more directly without the barrier of our egoic earthly mindset. Also, as we are connected seamlessly through the law of energy, we are inseparable from each other and will all experience the totality of the effects of individual and collective manifestations. Whatever we do unto others is in fact doing it unto ourselves in the Law of Oneness of the Universe. Our spirit would experience the same emotions as those we have interacted with, as well as others connected through the truth of love that created all of us.

My divine consciousness opened my heart to appreciate that my ex-husband had acted as a courageous hero in my life story. This spirit brother of mine subjected himself to the role of playing "bad" guy in order to enrich my learning experience on Earth. His spirit further humbled him by kneeling in front of the Heavenly Father and me to inspire my compassion. I was truly grateful to have the privilege to witness the beautiful grace from the Heavenly Father and my ex-husband.

Answers in the Light

I could not join Trudy the following Saturday, as I was still deeply affected by that unexpected and powerful encounter in the temple. I could hardly wait to call Trudy after the session, as I was anxious to ask her about the quality of light in the Celestial Room. I felt it was tremendously important to verify that I had not imagined anything. All Trudy said was, "The light was very dim this morning."

I finally stirred up enough courage to attend our regular Saturday temple session three weeks later. The familiar soft light was flowing into this beautiful room through the east windows. It was indeed much dimmer compared with that immeasurable brilliance of light before. Sitting on the sofa that morning, I remembered the powerful words that had come to me three weeks ago from the Heavenly Father, words that still ring in my heart to this day:

Remember, God's justice is different than human justice.

Each one of you is your own judge.

Experiencing spiritual remorse is much tougher than humans can visualize.

See, you are here with me and standing by my side.

Do Believe: Women and men are of the same value and importance in God's eyes.

Every one of you is cherished equally and loved unconditionally by God!

4

Archangel Michael and I

The Enchanted Waltz

s I approached the entrance hall at the spiritual retreat in July 2007, an impression urged me to stop at the restroom and get some tissues. It's a good thing that I listened to that prompting, even though I did not foresee what would happen. Soon after the session began, I saw a special message from Archangel Michael that filled the entire space of my spiritual vision. I was so overwhelmed that I collapsed into the most heart-wrenching sobs of my life. This moment confirmed the connection with Michael that was revealed on the night he first came to me.

Our First Date

On the very first day of July, I invited Archangel Michael to come into my presence that night. I told Michael that I wanted to meet him to make sure I was not being delusional about our relationship. Meeting at night during my sleep when my spirit was free to roam would be ideal. I had had out-of-body experiences many times in my life. Because of my exhaustion from the strange ordeal involving the archangels, I fell asleep and went into a deep trance-like state on that particular night.

Michael did show up for our date. I was quite surprised to see him greet me with a kiss and hug me tightly. *Do spirits kiss and hug each other like humans? How strange!* I thought. Our faces were translucent and gel-like, filled with billions of super-fine scintillating sparks of golden light. Michael expressed his exhilaration at having me in his arms by letting out a powerful, rolling roar of thunder. There was joyful melodic music when I expressed my own delight.

In the next scene, Michael led me to a room filled with bright white light in which the walls were lined with intricate compartments. He guided me over to a table with a book resting on its surface. When Michael opened the book to show me its contents, a bright gold light shot out from its pages. I was not allowed to see what was written in this book at the time. A few years later, I received confirmation that this book was one I would write to share the message of love with others (the book you are now reading).

Suddenly, my body was jerked awake by a tremendously loud crash. It sounded like a grand piano had been dropped from a tall building and slammed onto my floor. My heart was pounding rapidly, my ears were ringing loudly, and my head felt like a bomb had exploded inside of it from that thunderous crash. I was stunned and felt totally lost. It took me quite some time before I could sense my earthly surroundings. Tears streamed down my face uncontrollably. I felt as if something indescribably precious had been taken from me.

Returning from this spiritual encounter back to my earthly body was completely different from my previous out-of-body experiences. Usually, my spirit body had difficulty getting back into my physical form. It often took me considerable time and effort to connect the two together. This time, however, without any effort on my part, I was violently pushed back into my physical form after the meeting with Michael.

Nevertheless, ever since that encounter, sweet and gentle love saturates every breath I take, and every space of my world feels lovingly blessed. I had been given more than a taste of what it was like to be on "cloud nine." Everything around me seemed to have faded from sight. All that existed was the extraordinary richness of love. I could not stop my heart from singing with joy. The sensation was so sublime that I clung on to it, wishing it would never end. I perceived wholeness in me and around me, in everyone and everything. When Holly looked at me after this incident, she said that I looked and acted like those who are deeply in love.

My logical "scientific" mind was boggled. How was it possible to have such intense feelings for someone whose existence I could not prove, someone whom I could not even physically see or touch? And yet my undeniable feelings of love and connection with this being felt more real than my interactions with anyone or anything here on earth. The tender love and painful yearning flowed freely between us. I felt this loving connection express itself in everything, whether through my thoughts, my writing, my conversations, or seeing something I associated with him.

I realized that regardless of the ostensible distance between Heaven and Earth, there is no limit to our human ability to make a spiritual connection. There is no obstacle that can sever the shared love and communication between the Heavenly and earthly dimensions. The Universe is in our hands whenever we open our hearts to pure love.

Life with Michael in Heaven

In the upper level of the Heavenly home that Michael and I (as Aesina) shared, there was a "resting" room where we exchanged and processed our thoughts. What I noticed and truly liked was the ceiling. It opened to a view of the cosmos! We often flew up through the ceiling and traveled all over the Universe; sometimes pausing to hang suspended in space while enjoying each other's company.

There was a wide opening leading from the living room to a vast garden at the lower level. I did not see a door. Since there was no change of weather, nor any unfriendly intruders, partitions between the inside and outside were unnecessary.

However, there was a front door to the mansion. I am sure that privacy is respected in Heaven, too.

There was a beautiful pond that adorned the garden. White water lilies floated gracefully on its surface as if waltzing to music. Countless white flowers happily greeted each other in their fancy designer gowns. Most flower gardens would look quite boring without a variety of colors. The magical whiteness of this garden took me by surprise; its beauty reminded me of the Earth when covered with snow in the wintertime. My soul was in awe at the purity and peacefulness that a world of white could evoke. An impression came to me that the garden was created for me because white is my favorite color.

As I grew older, Michael and I often linked arms as we went for a leisurely stroll along the garden paths. We would discuss things, plan, and solve various issues in this beautiful setting. Much of my mentoring as I grew in spiritual wisdom was provided by Michael. He was always very understanding, patiently accepting my insatiable desire to learn and get to the heart of things. He always had a tender smile that uplifted my spirit whenever he looked at me. Those were such happy and precious moments!

Since we are made of energy, we can merge with other material forms, or even non-material things, to experience briefly what it's like to be that particular thing. I sometimes "hid" inside the ground and tickled Michael's feet from underneath or pulled him by his feet into the ground where he would merge with me. I also enjoyed stirring up ripples in the pond with my hands, as if running my fingers across the strings of a harp. Intricate music would thus be composed, which enticed the colorful fish to flip and wriggle in joyful dances.

My fun teasing Michael with energy was in fact his doing. He had inspired me. One day, as a little girl, I was playing with a small ball in the living room of my Heavenly home. As I pushed the ball on the floor with my short chubby arms, it grew bigger and bigger. Soon, the ball was so much larger than my body that I could hardly push it without getting buried underneath it. When young Michael saw my puzzled expression, he rolled on the floor with loud laughter. Michael had infused energy into the ball to tease me.

As I grew older, I gradually learned how to play with this energy. One time, while playing hide-and-seek with Michael, I became part of the large crystal sculpture standing at the left corner of the living room. He quickly discovered where I was and poked his finger in my tummy where the human belly button is located. His tickling triggered my giggles, which burst me out of the crystal sculpture. No matter how clever I was at hiding, I cannot recall a time when I outsmarted him.

Not only can we infuse energy into objects or merge with them, but we can also release and store our energy. One day, I saw myself lying on a crystal bed in the living room of Michael's and my Heavenly home. Brilliant golden light spurted out of the open door of a vault built with very thick walls. Somehow, I "just knew" that the energy of my memory, abilities, and character were being poured into and stored in this vault in preparation for my earthly life. Later, I mentioned to Holly that I had heard a crying sound during this vision. She said that it must have been Michael, who was sad that I had chosen not to take the memories of us in the Heavenly realm into my Earthly incarnation.

Signs from Michael

After our first date, many intense communications continued to come through from Michael for several months. One time, while driving on a street near the annual military airshow, I heard a loud voice above my head shout, "Michael!" as a jet airplane flew across the sky. I looked up and there was Michael, in military uniform, flying the aircraft. Connecting with him usually stirred up a complicated mix of feelings in me: pride, agony, and painful yearning. Once again, tears welled up from deep inside my heart. I could not help but weep all the way home.

Another one came after a long day of counseling clients at my office. I would unwind by listening to soft music on the radio while driving home. One day, as I reached for the dial, a very loud and clear voice said, "Michael," and reverberated inside the space of my car. If a name can carry commanding power, this was evidence! Moments later, I heard the most tender and loving voice of Michael himself: *"I miss you, too."* Perhaps he understood how tough things had been for me since finding out about our connection. It was as if his heart and thoughts had tuned in with mine, knowing how desperately I missed him. I managed to get home safely, despite the tears that blurred my eyes.

Messages in Songs

I continued to be frustrated about the situation with Michael and me, and yearned for him. At one point, a particular song I had not heard for decades kept ringing loudly in my head and followed me around for days. When I learned that the song was called "Send in the Clowns," I searched for the lyrics online. I was reduced to tears when I read the following words: "Are we a pair? Me here at last on the ground/You in midair . . . one who keeps tearing around . . . one who can't move . . ." Indeed, it was a frustrating situation to be stuck in a physical form with limited mobility, while he could roam through dimensions at will with his spirit body.

Another time, while surfing the Internet, something directed my attention to a video with a man singing opera at a small local festival in my native country. An unknown man started singing an Italian aria in front of folks who probably had never heard a song being sung in a foreign language, let alone a Western opera. By the time he reached the climax and sang the final word "vincero," I recognized the melody. It was "Nessun Dorma" from Puccini's *Turandot*.

I was moved to tears, once again, when I read the lyrics of this song:

". . . But my secret is hidden within me. . . At dawn, I will win! I will win!"

I remember asking Michael for months to let me know what he looked like when he came to Earth to help humans. He showed me by rapidly spinning the thousands of faces he took on Earth until I asked him to stop before my head got too dizzy. I wondered at the time if that was his playful answer to me. I still get sentimental when I hear this song so many years later.

We Are a Team

On my flight home from the spiritual retreat in July 2007, the captain announced that the flight would be very bumpy for the next two and a half hours due to the turbulent air current. The captain had tried unsuccessfully to fly above or around the current. Easily prone to motion sickness since childhood, I decided to test out the power of thought that I had just learned to alleviate the situation. I imagined wrapping my arms around the entire plane in order to stabilize it. The plane got less bumpy, but it was still unsteady. I asked Michael for help. He instantly showed up and extended his arms to join mine so we could wrap the entire plane together. An inspiration urged me to blow open a tunnel in front of the plane. Surprisingly, the plane stabilized within minutes, as if flying through this tube in a void. To this day, I am still amazed at how the flight remained smooth for the rest of the journey. I also cannot forget Michael's reassuring words: "We are a team. We work together."

His White Light

Michael always announced his presence to me with bright white light, mostly on my left side. There were times when I was jerked out of a deep slumber by an exceedingly brilliant light that seemed to explode in my bedroom. It would take a few seconds to calm my pounding heart from these astonishing visits. If this grand-scale explosion of energy happened in the physical and not the spiritual realm, it would cause tremendous damage. I usually felt quite lost when the room went back to the same dark state as the world outside my windows. The immense love I felt coming from the light during these experiences shook my soul, and usually brought tears for days afterward.

I now understand that spirits can become overly zealous without the experience of an earthly body's physical response. Sometimes Michael would flicker his light rapidly until I had to ask him to please stop his mischief before it gave me a headache. At other times, I had to ask him to "dim his light" as he hung above my head so I could rest or sleep better.

Heart Hugs

For several months after my first encounter with Michael, I had been having irregular heartbeats and feeling a powerful thumping on my sternum. The thumping often made it hard for me to talk, and I felt as if I was choking when the thumping was most deliberate. I suspected that Michael was somehow involved, because it happened whenever Holly and I asked him for confirmation about spiritual issues, or when I had questions about the Heavenly realm. I decided to visit my doctor to make sure I was not being delusional or suffering from an unknown physical ailment.

At the doctor's office, a nurse checked my blood pressure, pulse, and heartbeat. Everything on my chart read within the normal range; I was even healthier than most people. The thumping on my sternum had been persistent and especially strong that morning, so I asked the nurse to double check my heart rate. I heard the same comment as at my prior checkups: "You have the heartbeat of a healthy athlete." Yet I still felt the sensation of powerful, rapid thumping, so I asked the doctor to measure my heartbeat and examine my heart more carefully. Once again, I got the comment about how strong and healthy my heart was.

I had asked Michael to make it clear beyond any doubt when he wanted to connect with me by using hard-to-miss signs and signals. Evidently, he had chosen one of the most obvious methods to get my attention. I wondered if he was enjoying himself and having a hearty laugh to see me flustered and with a flushed face.

I confess that not until witnessing the Heavenly Parents' Creation of the Spirits would I realize that the sternum was the location of our "spirit heart." It seems Michael had been attempting to connect with me heart-to-heart!

Vibrational Tease

Since childhood, I have felt strong tingly sensations in my body at times. I thought everyone had feelings like that. So, I never gave it a second thought when I started to experience these sensations more frequently about the time Michael appeared in my life. However, as time went by, and an electric-like current ran through my physical body and continued to get stronger, I started piecing it all together. I am certain that Michael was using this method to make his presence known, because the vibration would arise and increase when I was barely awake in the morning or when I was alone. Michael perhaps figured that he could best get my attention when I was not distracted by daily activities.

I noticed that most of the time the vibration would start in the center of my chest, and the current would spread all over my body, from the top of my head to the tips of my fingers and toes. Sometimes, the vibration would get so strong that I couldn't move my arms. Other times, the powerful vibrations seemed to lift my body a few inches above the bed and made me feel like one of those floating bodies in the magic shows. There were moments when I thought the powerful current would jerk me out of my bed.

At times, the vibration felt strong and persistent on certain sections of my head for days. My hair would rise from my scalp and move with the vibration. I couldn't find a logical explanation for this since there was never a draft or static electricity. Whenever this happened, I would pat down my hair to make the mischievous tingling, which could be quite annoying, go away. But the vibration had a will of its own and wouldn't stop until it'd had fun on different parts of my scalp. It was naughty of Michael for daring to mess up a lady's hair, ha ha.

Gifts from Michael

The Veil

For the life of me, I could never have believed it possible to feel so excited about receiving invisible gifts, or so grateful. One afternoon, Michael popped into my vision just after I had closed my eyes, desperate for a nap. He took me to a beach with a beautiful sunset over the ocean and waves rippling softly underneath the darkening sky. Next, I was surprised to see shimmering moons and stars floating on the ocean. Before logic could step in and insist that the moons and stars should be in the sky instead of the ocean, Michael did something that I will never forget for the rest of my life.

Suddenly, within the palms of his hands, there appeared a lovely transparent veil adorned with glittering stars and moons. He had made a veil out of the water of the ocean, the moons, and the stars! He draped the veil tenderly around my head and let the long ends trail softly down my back to the floor. This exquisitely beautiful veil hugged my shoulders and lovingly caressed my face. It was a classic gesture of romance.

Sleepiness had left me completely by then. I was alert and revitalized with amazement. With a big grin, Michael told me that he was simply showing me his love with a gift, just like a human lover would do. I am sure his beaming smile came from knowing that no man on earth could have made a scarf out of the ocean, stars, and moons.

The White Rose

I will never forget the very first gift I received from Michael. On the last day of July 2007, a clear and strong impression suddenly popped into my mind, completely unrelated to the book I was reading at bedtime: *It was Michael who sent me that white rose.* This impression was so strong that it struck me like an absolute confirmation.

This unexpected message blew open a gate closed long ago, and fiery feelings filled my entire being. I burst into tears. All I could do was to choke out repeatedly: "Oh, my God! Oh, my God!"

Years earlier, in October 1995, after singing in my graduation music recital, I was presented with many bouquets of flowers by my family and friends. The most memorable was a single, twenty-four-inch, long-stemmed white rose. It was the first such rose I had ever received. I was enchanted by the refreshing purity and stunning beauty of this rose. A powerful and peculiar sensation struck my heart when I read the words on the note card enclosed with the rose. If I remember correctly, it read, "When you speak, God listens; when you sing, God smiles."

The card had no name on it. For two years afterwards, I tried to find the person who had given me the white rose, but to no avail. People told me that a white rose symbolizes "death." Nevertheless, I felt alive and invigorated by its pure, vibrant energy. It has been my favorite type of flower ever since.

The Necklace

One day in a vision, I saw Michael happily dangling something shiny in the shape of a necklace before me. He told me that it was a gift. I said to him jokingly, "How would you give it to me? By magic?" A vision appeared, answering for him. I saw Michael and Holly in a large conference room where the Heavenly Parents and the other archangels conducted their meetings; they were gathered closely together with their heads bent down, as if conspiring something in secrecy.

A few days later, I opened my door to a very excited Holly. She had brought with her a beautiful red jewelry box, which she handed to me. Inside, sitting serenely on the red cushion, was an exquisitely delicate necklace made of sky-blue Swarovski crystals of the best quality. There were seven blue stars intended to represent the seven years between Michael's and my age. Holly told me that if it weren't for Michael's inspiration, she would not have been able to connect the stars on the necklace so successfully. I was moved to tears by Holly's kindness, generosity, and love. She graciously said, "It is not from me. It is Michael's gift to you."

Holly told me to try on the necklace to see if the length fit me. As soon as I took the necklace out of the jewelry box, we both felt a strong electric current running through us. Because of the powerful energy, Holly lost her balance. Giggling from the unexpected tingles of electricity, Holly looked for a place to sit down and steady herself. With a hand gesture, she made "shu shu" sounds, in the attempt to describe how the electric current went through her whole body. She said, "You must have activated the power and energy of this necklace."

I was inspired to hold the necklace against my forehead at the location of the "third eye" (in the middle of the forehead above and between the eyebrows). As soon as the necklace touched my head, bright light instantly flared out from it with intense love. For years, the necklace let out exuberant love waves whenever I held it in my hand.

Dancing Crystals

Sometimes Michael would let us know ahead of time that he had a gift in store for Holly and me that day. This type of message usually triggered lots of giggling as we had fun guessing what the gift might be. I suspected that Michael derived much joy from creating the suspense and watching these two silly old ladies acting like schoolgirls.

One afternoon, Holly and I were sitting on a bench beside the ocean. I had my eyes closed as I relaxed in the warm sun. Suddenly, Holly shrieked with delight. I could not help but scream with excitement too when I looked in awe at the ocean. There in front of us, a long path of about thirty feet wide, paved with golden sparkles like millions of shining crystals, stretched all the way to the horizon. This golden path was bordered on both sides by a purple light (purple usually represented Michael). The crystals danced joyfully to the rhythm of the ocean waves, as the gold and purple ribbons of light streamed along gracefully. Like the finale of a fireworks display, a giant chandelier arose and hung above the middle of this golden path. This exquisite grand chandelier burst into thousands of brilliant golden rays of light. No words could adequately describe this spectacular presentation. Our hearts were full of gratitude for this amazing gift of love.

Coffee Treat

Holly and I had assumed that spirits do not succumb to the same temptations and shallow concerns as we humans. We considered them lucky not to have to deal with their figure and weight issues or be concerned about making fashion statements with their clothing. However, as time went by, we became more and more convinced that spirits do have preferences for certain favorite things in the world where humans reside.

Upon our inquiring, Michael would let Holly and I know what he preferred during our outings, which usually consisted of strolling, dining out, and shopping. We were surprised how often he mentioned that he liked coffee and chocolate. "How can a spirit like what humans like?" I said to Holly, who was as surprised as I was to hear it. I realized much later that since all beings are connected through energy, spirits can receive sensations through our human experiences. Each spirit has its own unique attributes, therefore, its favorites.

One day, Michael said with a beaming smile that he would treat Holly and me to coffee. *Hmmm . . .* I thought. *How would he treat us to earthly stuff without earthly cash or plastic?* The restaurant where we went for lunch by the sea was quite busy that day. The service was very slow, and our waiter simply disappeared after we placed our order. More than half an hour later, the manager approached and said he would provide the coffee of our choice, free of charge, as a gesture of apology.

Michael offered to treat Holly and me to coffee on yet another occasion. From our last experience, we were looking forward to seeing the ingenious plan that Michael would come up with this time. Holly and I met at a shopping mall and waited anxiously all day for Michael to appear, but to no avail. We decided to leave the mall when it was getting dark.

As Holly and I were walking toward the parking garage of the mall, we passed by a kitchenware store that was about to close for the evening. We quickly went into the store to buy something for Holly's kitchen. While Holly was paying for her purchase, the cashier asked us if we would like to try some coffee. This was puzzling, as we did not smell the aroma of brewed coffee. The cashier showed us a new coffee maker that the store was going to promote next morning. She invited us to pick whatever flavors we liked from the assorted coffee pods. We were the first ones to use this new machine and the last customers before they closed the shop.

Love Proclaimed

My life has been truly blessed by the gift of Archangel Michael's loving presence, to have him by my side as my Heavenly mate. A Heavenly mate is different from a "soul mate." Everyone can have a number of soul mates; spirit brothers and sisters that play different roles to help us learn, grow, evolve, and expand our soul. Whereas a Heavenly mate is like a "pairing" created by our Heavenly Parents for a particular spirit for certain purposes. Michael has taught me the meaning of unconditional love. With Michael, I feel completely respected, cherished, and safe to be my human self. I experience no guilt or shame for my mistakes, nor do I feel the need to hide my weaknesses and imperfections from him. He understands the value and accepts the expression of my character that I have chosen for my human experiences.

Whenever I ask Michael how to repay him for his kindness or make him happy, he says, "Just be happy!" It took me a long time to finally understand the significance of those three simple words. We are the energy of light and love that illuminates the world with boundless bliss, serene beauty, and passionate joy. This divine happiness not only affects us individually when we're in a state of inner peace. Our happiness, in turn, affects all that IS. More joy creates more joy! It is an ingenious "win-win," "happy-happy" design!

I no longer feel the need either to conceal or prove the existence of my relationship with Michael to the world. I am ready to share the words of the message I received from him at the retreat in 2007 when a gigantic banner filled my field of vision:

The Loving Connection

My Love for you

is ETERNAL

No Beginning   No End

5

Everlasting Love

The Gift of My Children

I will always remember a special encounter with the Heavenly light in 1977. I was suffering from diarrhea due to an unknown cause. After weeks of not being able to keep food in me, I was so weak that I could not get out of bed. I could feel the life force slipping out of me as my body turned colder and colder, even underneath thick blankets in the hot humid summer of Tehran, Iran. All I could do was plead in my thoughts: *Help me, God. I am dying.*

No sooner had the plea taken place in my thoughts than I saw a dot of extremely bright, golden light appear high above me, as if the ceiling were nonexistent. It flew toward me and landed between my eyebrows. As soon as the light hit me, I felt a soothing coolness, and I immediately fell into a very deep sleep.

Two hours later when I woke up, I was amazed that I felt truly well and quite refreshed, even energetic. All the signs of dehydration and weakness had miraculously disappeared. A voice urged me to go to an obstetrician/gynecologist for a checkup. Lo and behold, I was pregnant with my first child, a son!

I thank God every day for sending this beautiful, kind, good-natured, and loving spirit into my life. To begin his fun, he announced his arrival with a fanfare of three powerful kicks to break open the amniotic sac. Of course, I must also mention how smart and good-looking he is (I swear by the heart of his mother to its truth...*wink, wink*). Besides being highly intelligent, humorous, and talented, he has demonstrated integrity, thoughtfulness, generosity, and compassion since the time he was a little child. Family and friends can always count on him to offer his support and share his benevolence.

A second beautiful blessing came to me with the birth of my daughter. It was sad to see my son playing all by himself when he was a toddler, so I prayed to the Heavenly Father to bring him a sister. I also wanted to experience having a daughter. Within two weeks, I knew I was pregnant, and my doctor soon confirmed the good news. When I asked the Heavenly Father if it was a girl, an electrical current vibrated powerfully through my whole body for nearly three days in answer to my question. Intense joy permeated my entire being, just like when I was pregnant with my first child. Happy smiles seemed to be "glued" permanently on my face. I frequently hummed little jolly tunes I made-up while dreaming about what my baby girl would look like and what kind of disposition she would have. I felt no guilt but giggled with delight when shopping for lots of cute baby girls' clothing.

My daughter was born exactly two weeks before her due date, and on an even day as I had requested in a prayer. I wanted to give myself enough time to get physically strong for my parents' visit. I still remember her perfectly round face and large eyes filled with curiosity when she met this world. Not only was she gifted with the same fine qualities and artistic talents as her brother, but she could also turn heads with her exotic beauty and touch hearts with her loving kindness. She often brought us to tears laughing at her one-of-a-kind humor and goofiness.

I am truly grateful and happy to have witnessed my son and daughter get along so well and support each other throughout their lives and grow up to be such amazing people.

The Wheel of Life

Fast forward to many years later . . . I hadn't seen my grown daughter for quite some time. I was thrilled that she was coming over to drop something off from my son. I decided to make it a special occasion and had prepared a nice dinner for us. But after all my anticipation, she called to say she couldn't make it but would come by the following day.

Knowing that my daughter did not like leftovers, I went to the supermarket the next day to get fresh ingredients. I also bought a pot of beautiful orchids for her. I was filled with excitement and joy when I heard the doorbell ring that evening. When I opened the door and stretched out my arms to hug her, my daughter kept her distance. She refused my invitation to dine together. She laid down the bag from my son on the ground by the door, instead of handing it to me, and said, "I did not ask you to cook for me. You cannot make me, neither am I going to feel guilty."

Stunned by her cold ungrateful remarks, so unlike the daughter I knew, I tried to find out the cause of her bitterness and anger. She became indignant and accused me of accepting monetary assistance from my sister for years and of burdening my son financially. She also told me that the damage I had done to her was too much and too painful to explain. The last words I heard from her as she walked away stung me to my core: "There is no basis for us to build any relationship on. I am just fine having the same arrangement with you that I have with dad."

She had been estranged from her dad for years, and now it was my turn to be cast out of her life. In a desperate attempt to soften her heart, choking with tears, I declared my love to her as she started descending the stairs outside my door. "If I die tomorrow, I want you to know you are well-loved by your mother. If I die tomorrow, I want you to know I have tried my best to be a good mother." I watched her walk away until her silhouette faded into the distance.

What happened? How could there be NO relationship between us? Where is the love we had shared? I was confused and devastated. My whole being was crushed by anguish. I now understood how someone could die of a broken heart. Despite my suffering, my thoughts went to my daughter. I wondered whether she would eat some food and take a good rest after her hard day of work at the office. I hoped she had found some peace from her challenging confrontation.

The Value of Money

Even though I have never been well off financially, I have managed to live a comfortable life free of debt. Not only have I taken care of my own expenses, but I have also helped my children and my brother and his daughters in times of need, and I give to charity. While my daughter was living with her father during my graduate school education, I provided child support. I also often helped her out financially even after she was independent.

My sister is known for her compassion and generosity. Her charitable spirit is truly praiseworthy. She has always been devoted to our family members, especially our parents, and often gives monetary gifts for birthdays and special occasions. It came as a surprise to me, however, when she generously contributed toward my tuition for graduate school. I repaid her kindness with the skills and knowledge received from my professional training. I also wrote her a letter expressing my sincere gratitude when I reimbursed her a few years ago.

My son is successful financially. In view of my many physical challenges, my son provided generous financial gifts that enabled me to retire from my stressful career. He declined any repayment, assuring me that it was not a burden but an honor to take care of me and make me happy. In a heartfelt letter, he thanked me for raising him and credited me for his goodness, saying that he wished to continue to share his good fortune with me. Other family members, including his sister, have been recipients of my son's generosity. Friends and strangers have also been the beneficiaries of his kindness.

My daughter has always worked very hard, as she believes that a person's value is judged by their services to others and financial independence. Understandably, she has contempt for "freeloaders" who shamelessly piggyback on other people's hard work and charity. She was upset to see how I enjoyed being treated to fine dining and receiving nice gifts from wealthy friends. In fact, I often felt ashamed of my enjoyment of materialistic pleasures myself.

Now older and wiser, I must thank my daughter for transforming my concept about money. I now recognize that spirituality embraces the joy and abundance of the Universe, and to believe that hardship and suffering are necessary for us is egoic thinking. Rather than being stuck in the belief that "the love of money is the root of all evil," I can honor money as a sacred tool made with the beautiful energy of love and wisdom. It provides us opportunities to learn how to give and receive with wisdom, knowing when and how to best use this valuable resource. It supports our spiritual evolution by shifting an egoic mindset to one of selfless intention. We can use this powerful resource to serve others with love. Giving with a heartfelt intention is an act of love, and to receive gifts with joy and gratitude honors the giver. Love is kept alive through proper flowing and balancing.

Calling for Love

While writing about the day when my daughter and I parted ways, other tormenting memories flashed through my mind. I recalled that during the two years before that incident, my daughter had cringed whenever I hugged her. She would look at me with disgust when I said it was a privilege to be a mother. One day, she confessed the reason for her change of heart. She told me that by leaving her behind with her dad after the divorce, I had proved that I did not want her. She was convinced that she must have been an accident, an unwanted child. Trapped in this belief, she no longer allowed family and friends to celebrate her birthday, as it would only deepen her pain. In truth, I had thought my daughter would be better off to stay in her familiar home surroundings, and I felt she would have a more comfortable life with her dad, who had financial stability. I also had believed her dad would be a responsible and caring father.

How sad that a wounded heart can grow into an angry flame and destroy someone's peace and happiness. Before the divorce, my then-husband and I had provided our son and daughter with a happy, comfortable, home life. We never subjected our children to any kind of physical or mental abuse, nor did we pressure them with our own expectations. We were involved in their studies and extracurricular activities, and we exposed them to diverse cultural events. We also provided them with abundant opportunities to follow their dreams and develop their potential.

How I cherished the times when my daughter wanted to cuddle up with me in bed and chat for hours. I felt honored when she asked me to care for her during her times of need. Tears welled up as I reminisced about our happy times shopping, dining, and strolling in street fairs together. We often exchanged funny instant messages that brought much laughter. How grateful I was for the precious gifts that she designed for me or bought with her meager budget.

I remember back in 2006 when my daughter and I had to cut short a visit with my mom in Hawaii and fly back to California to take care of the aftereffects from a breakup with her boyfriend. After only a few hours of sleep in three days, I drove straight through from Northern to Southern California to bring her home to live with me. Suffering as I do from severe motion sickness and spinal injuries, traveling in any kind of vehicle is a challenge for me. However, my lifelong fear and "vehicular disability" lost its grip on me as I drove up and down the winding hills that used to frighten me even as a passenger. All I could think about was easing my daughter's pain any way I could. It was the first (and last) time in my life that I would drive such a long distance. I was super powered by a mother's love.

I was truly happy and grateful to have this second chance to care for my daughter after the divorce. I worked exceptionally hard to give us a comfortable life and helped her continue her college studies. More than anything, I hoped to heal her broken heart with a mother's love and devotion.

Where did all this love go?

During the year after the traumatic break with my daughter, I sent her many texts and email messages expressing my love and concern. I also selected meaningful gifts, beautifully wrapped, for my son to give her. I asked him to give her extra hugs for me whenever they met. Sadly, I never received a response from her. So, I decided to write a letter and let her know that her life was a precious gift from God, the answer to my prayer. I shared the story of my emotional state in my marital relationship, and I explained that in order to avoid subjecting her and her brother to an unhealthy family environment, I chose to get a divorce from her dad. I humbly apologized for causing her so much pain and for my inability to protect her. I also sincerely thanked her for all that she had done for me. I told her how proud I was that she had turned out to be such a courageous, responsible, ethical, and loving young woman.

The days, months, and years passed. As far as I know, all of my efforts to reconcile with her have been in vain.

The Blossoming of Self-Love

After my daughter's departure in March 2014, the guilt and grief continued to torment me for not being the kind of mother my daughter could trust or be proud of. In May 2015, I heard a loud voice and saw these words hanging midair: *There is no need for you to feel guilty or to apologize to her anymore.* The concept of "self-love" entered my radar soon afterward.

Through years of ongoing learning and practices, I came to see that self-love is a sacred mechanism to purify and transform our humanness for a deeper connection with our soul. Cultivating self-love empowers us to vitalize our physical form, clarify our mind, master heart-coherence, and lead us home to the unlimited powerful divine being that we truly are. It is not a quick fix of egoic gratification or narcissistic self-interest, but altruistic self-care to explore, accept, honor, care for, and appreciate who and what we are: the perfect divine love!

To harvest the sweet fruit of self-love takes dedicated commitment and diligent practice. No blame or excuses. Be curious but not judgmental. We must take responsibility for our own contribution to all that disturbs our inner peace and face the root cause of our fear, imbalance, disharmony, and brokenness. We also need to step out of our comfort zone. And we need to learn how to set boundaries when it comes to love for ourselves and those with whom we interact. To move self-love forward, we have to be kind, gentle, forgiving, and patient with our own progress. Slips, trips, and falls are inevitable. That is when we need to hug ourselves with loving understanding. It is time to relax and take a brief break. Recommit and practice again. One breath at a time.

Deprograming those beliefs that make us feel unvalued, unloved, and powerless can unshackle our uniqueness and greatness. Releasing our anger, resentment, or self-judgment, and staying clear of those people, situations, and substances that drain our energy will allow us to live a dynamic and effective life. Abundance of love and joy will rush into every cell of our being when we no longer live in the bondage of fear, scarcity, and limitation.

It is so freeing to stop basing our identification and worth upon external approval and validation. Nevertheless, the outer world is the projection and reflection of our inner self. When our emotions and our mind run amok and trigger our judgmental bias against others, this can trap us in the state of "dis-ease," and cause us to retreat to our familiar zone of smallness. This alerts us to turn inward and nurture this pure love to rectify that issue.

Self-love also leads us to honor and accept our physical form and that of others. Our physical body is an energy form of supreme intelligence with amazing functionality that is always responding to our emotions and sending us messages from our higher self. We need to be respectful to this sacred vessel by keeping it clean and in good order, so that we can learn, grow, and enjoy our earthly experiences with optimal vitality and health. We also need to appreciate and facilitate the gifts of illness, pain, and suffering, as they awaken us to deeper wisdom and love.

Pure love embodies the elements of unconditionality, gratitude, and wisdom. It does not associate with "if," "should," or "expectations," but encourages us to evaluate the "who, when, how, and what" to offering love. It is not easy to love myself unconditionally in view of my weaknesses and imperfections, not to mention loving those who blatantly cause harm to others. I came to the realization that when we raise our awareness to the state of loving Oneness, we are able to recognize that each spirit was created with the divine spark of unconditional love, gratitude, and wisdom. We certainly need not like, condone, or agree with ugliness or darkness. However, connecting to pure love, we will have empathy and compassion even for those who act from ignorance and hurt others. Our hearts will be filled with gratitude for the wisdom embedded in the intricate design of life.

The more we surrender to the grace of love, the more easily we can stand up for our truth and serve this truth with integrity. Through this process of grounding and raising our spiritual consciousness, we can remember our truth and live as magnificent, powerful beings of light and love. I am so grateful that by learning to love myself, I can gradually acknowledge my truth while also honoring that of others.

The Daughter in the Mirror

Like my own daughter, I had a ghost to deal with as a child. The birth of a daughter in my traditional culture was not considered as desirable as having a son. My parents were not influenced by that bias, and they were open-minded compared with most. However, I had an older sister and a younger brother, so I was affected by the middle-child syndrome, which intensified feelings of unworthiness, insecurity, and not being "good enough." Even though I would laugh at myself often, and always felt much joy from seeing other people laughing happily with my buffoonery, I was often tormented by the dread of making mistakes and offending or displeasing others. I feared people in general.

I still remember the way my aunt looked at me when she urged my parents to give this "money-losing" female child away. I had heard countless horrible stories about the inhumane abuse and torture of young girls given away or sold by their parents, including my aunt's own daughter and some elementary classmates. Most of them met an early death in unspeakably horrid ways. Unfortunately, being taught to be submissive and obedient, it never entered my young mind to question why there were no laws to halt such prevalent shameful practices. As far as I know, there were no viable programs to assist families in financial need and save their daughters from being given away at that time.

The fear and guilt of being a burdensome daughter drove me to be a people pleaser. I would even blame myself when something went wrong that was not my fault. I also believed that I had to excel in all possible areas in order to prove to my family, friends, and the world that I was worth keeping. Consequently, as mistakes, failures, and heartaches accumulated throughout my life, my terror of being unloved deepened, and I always felt in danger of revealing my flaws.

I felt justified to blame my mother as the source of my self-critical perfectionism, along with most of my failures. I admit that I was not a perfect child. During my early childhood, there were many purple welts on my little body from my mom's beatings, and that brought a few visits from my schoolteachers to talk to my mom. Physical discipline of children was culturally acceptable for parents and teachers at the time. I remember feeling devastated by the cold, unreasonable remark my mother made when I told her I had received a scholarship for excellent academic achievement that would pay for my high school tuition: "I don't see cash in my hand."

Most intolerable was her near-daily reminder that I was an "inconsiderate, money-wasting, selfish girl" for wanting to attend college rather than go to the vocational school like my sister. My guilt was mixed with fury, since my sister's teachers had persuaded my mom to let me pursue the traditional educational route of high school and college. Subsequently, even though I succeeded in passing the extremely tough entrance examination and entered the most prestigious university in my country, I felt no pride, only sadness.

I was also aggrieved by my mom's lack of appreciation for my musical talents. When I excitedly told her that I was one of the two students in my junior high school who had been chosen to study music in Vienna, Austria, my friend for piano, and I for singing, she said, "That is a waste of money and for no good." Negative comments such as this had traumatized me for years. I never felt accomplished, even though I had procured grants, stayed on the Dean's list, and later graduated at the top of my class as a music major from a university in northern California. To attain this degree, I had to weather a tough divorce, endure daily intense pain (from whiplash and a cracked tailbone), and struggle to understand the English language, my third language, after Taiwanese and Mandarin Chinese. Doubting my ability to succeed, I did not accept an invitation to study music in Italy on a Fulbright Scholarship. I also turned down a grant that two professors offered me to refine my musical training at Stanford University. Remorse and regret would sadden me for decades afterward from my wounded ego.

During high school, I ran away from home for a few days in order to get away from my mother's criticism. Such a rebellious act against one's parents was nearly unheard of in my culture during that time. Looking at my mom's hurt expression later, I was sure she had read what I had written in my journal: "She only loves my sister and brother. She is so mean to me. I wonder if she is my 'real' mother." Immersed in my misery and anger, despite the humiliation and pain I had brought on her, my hardened heart refused to show her any compassion. I had made her "lose face" in front of our neighbors as a failed mother.

Later, while at the university in Taiwan, my college roommates bullied me, which further magnified my despair. I was determined to end my pathetic life once and for all. During the winter break, I waited until all my roommates had left the dorm. Then I swallowed over a hundred pills of different kinds: for sleeping aid, allergies, colds, diarrhea, etc. I sliced the cubital veins on my arm and the radial artery on my wrist to make sure I would not come back. But somehow, I survived. I was puzzled as to why soft white clouds had appeared and wrapped thickly around me. (I later found out from various sources that angels could present themselves as energy clouds.) Strangely, hardly any blood had spurted from the deep cuts, nor did my stomach need to be pumped.

My worried parents rushed to my side after learning about my failed suicide attempt. However, the deep concern on their faces was powerless to warm my cold, desolate heart. The only thought that shot through my emotional void was, *I really hate being alive . . .*

Encased in the egoic small-self-syndrome, I could not understand then and not until decades later, that the shortcut I took to end my miseries was in fact stemming from the absence of self-love. Lacking spiritual maturity, I did not see the ripple effects of the consequences of my actions that signified the lack of compassion for myself. Unbeknown to me at the time, all our experiences, whether gentle or harsh, are the careful, intelligent, and loving design of our soul to open our heart to love through the process of healing our traumas and adjusting our energy to divine harmony. There are different degrees of intensity, various methods, and lengths of time needed for healing and adjustment. It all depends on how much work is involved; whether we are healing just for our personal issues in the current and/or past lives, or for our families and communities, or even including for the whole of humanity.

So, I found yet another escape route by getting married one year before my college graduation and moving to America with my then-husband. After failing to convince me to stay until I had graduated from the university in Taiwan, people shook their heads and sighed, "What a pity." Even my university was stunned by my decision, as hardly any student in my country would ever give up this much sought-after and hard-to-get "golden diploma."

All the pent-up emotion and anger against my mom finally blew up when I was around thirty years old. Even though I visited my parents in Taiwan only once or twice a year after my marriage, my mom still used it as an opportunity to accuse me of being a "selfish" daughter. I screamed at her for the irreparable damage she had done to me; I blamed her for my character flaws, misfortunes, mistakes, and sorrows. I also blamed her for my co-dependency and lack of boundaries, for my low self-esteem and insecurity.

I was sick with fright, as this was the first time that I had ever dared to speak out against anyone. And I felt awful about it, because good children should not retort or argue and especially should not raise their voice against their parents. I had committed an unforgivable sin condemned by Heaven and Earth in my culture. And yet after my outburst, my mom never scorned me or called me selfish again; nor did she ever criticize anyone else. Surprisingly, my mom and I began to share life moments, likes and dislikes, laughter and tears, openly and intimately. She never failed to support me with patience, understanding, and great wisdom, and she often spiced things up with her fun personality. Our love was no longer limited to the mother and daughter relationship. We became true friends!

Out of the Cocoon

I have always believed that both ignorance and arrogance create the kind of pathology that causes the chaos and tragedy in people's lives. I also understand how dangerous and deceptive false beliefs held as truth can be. However, I was deeply trapped in such folly myself for many years and could not escape from my self-destructive conditioning. My egoic mind had interpreted my world with fear-based and limited beliefs. My emotional and spiritual immaturity had prevented me from accepting my mom's egoic struggles and having to deal with life challenges like any other human being. Consequently, I was blinded by my own misery and felt no gratitude toward my mother for her incredible devotion to me and my family.

Not only did we live in one of the most beautiful homes on our street, but my mother had also decorated its interior with her design talents. She also cooked us nutritious and delicious meals and made plenty of tasty homemade snacks. We children were well dressed in beautiful and stylish handmade clothing that invited praise from others. Family and friends showered their admiration and praise on my mom. They made good use of the knowledge she shared with them about science, medicine, the economy, and politics. She also had amazing skills for household repairs.

A few years after my confrontation with my mom, I could understand and appreciate why she had frequently criticized me in front of my sister and others for being selfish. Perhaps she had only pretended to be convinced by my sister's teachers to let me attend regular high school, when in fact she had been forced into making a decision she regretted and resented. To appease my sister, my mom constantly praised her as being the better daughter, and she thanked my sister for her "sacrifice" in attending the vocational school. The graduates trained at the vocational schools were ready to join the workforce and produce income for their families in just three years. Unfortunately, attending such schools was not as well-regarded as the traditional high school and college route that promised higher social status and earning potential. My wonderful sister never complained but generously served our family and those in need with the excellent financial management skills from her vocational training.

Love Never Dies

Thinking about my dad always brings me happy and grateful smiles. My dad was a loving husband and father who worked hard to provide our family with a very comfortable life. I admired his great integrity, compassion, intelligence, and humor. His artistic and musical talents were an inspiration to me. Most of all, I miss how he cherished and loved me unconditionally. He was my safe harbor and will forever be my hero.

It became clear in November 2003, from the complications resulting from a surgical procedure, that my dad would soon be departing from this world. In the weeks before he crossed over, we noticed that his attention was fixed on a spot near the ceiling. He would stare at it for hours, oblivious to what was happening around him. His facial expression was lively, and his lips moved as if conversing with someone. It took a strong effort to draw his awareness back to earthly reality.

On November 30, my mom gave the doctor permission to remove my dad's life support when his kidney failed him. While the doctor was pulling out the many tubes, I encouraged my dad to follow the light and go home to a carefree world where he could enjoy his favorite hobbies: reading and drawing. My dad had always loved to hear me sing, so I sang to him through my terrible sadness until he closed his eyes in peace. The sight of the tears running down my dad's cheeks, knowing that he would soon be leaving his beloved family, was heartbreaking. This memory would torment me forever.

Even during the last moments of his life, my dad was just as thoughtful as always. Gathering the last ounce of strength, he still managed to adjust his already weakened body to make it easier for the doctor to pull out the tubes and for my sister to dress him afterward. I was not prepared for the amount of respect and love he would receive from others. I lost count of the number of people who brought meals and visited my dad every day during his three months in the hospital. Many were from the charitable organizations that my dad and mom had served for years. Long after his departure from Earth, those who knew and loved him still talked about my dad's unsurpassed integrity and kindness as a bank executive.

My dad was my role model. Unpretentious and low key, he never showed off his awards for his artwork. His drawings were selected to represent our country in an international art exhibition in New York City, a rare honor at the time. As he also never bragged about his noble deeds, I found out from my mom about the many lives he had made better during his lifetime. When I was in elementary school, I was confused to see a man come to our home every night for a couple of years; he would come after dinner and stay to talk with my father even after I went to bed. My mom later explained that my dad was teaching this man how to handle the job that he had secured for him at the bank where my dad was an executive.

I also remember a man who lived in poverty in one of the streets behind my childhood home. He confided to my dad that he was contemplating suicide to avoid the shame of imprisonment for embezzlement. In desperation to feed his family, he had stolen money from his company. Without a second thought, my dad borrowed the funds to pay back this man's company. Years later, this man brought his children to thank my dad, saying, "If not for you, I would not have been able to survive in society as my reputation would have been ruined. My children would not have had a father to grow up with. It would have been horrible for my wife to care for our children and my elderly mother alone."

How I miss singing, dancing, whistling, and playing sports with my dad, as well as listening to him play different musical instruments. In my early childhood, I was often engrossed in reading the popular comic books that my dad himself had written and illustrated. I will always remember how he entertained us like a clown, totally unleashed from the dignified image expected from a man of his status. My dad would do almost anything for his beloved family, even though he was generally shy and reserved.

And now, this great man, who had raised me with his generous love and nurtured me in security with his never-failing support, was lying lifeless on the hospital bed. Gone . . . My heart ached with pain, and I could not stop sobbing.

Soon, my dad's hospital room was filled with members of my parents' charitable organization. They had come to assist my dad in crossing over with a Buddhist chant. Incredulously, my dad's lifeless face became radiant and peaceful, even the age spots on his face were fading away, as the chanting of the members continued. For years afterward, my mom loved to share this miracle story with anyone willing to listen.

Six hours into the chanting ceremony, I saw my dad's spirit body standing about three feet at the right side of the head of the bed. His spirit body was wearing a long white robe, not the traditional embroidered Chinese robe that my sister had put on him. He was confused to see his lifeless physical body and all those people chanting in his hospital room. It only took a few seconds for understanding to dawn and clear away his bewilderment. He became calm and joyous.

I always smile when I remember what he said to me after rising from his earthy form:

"What an exhausting journey this time!"

Indeed, my dad had had an extremely tough childhood and suffered tremendous health challenges throughout his earthly life.

Immediately after adapting to his new surroundings, he said to me, "I love you. Please let your sister know I love her too." My sister was sitting next to me among the chanting members.

He then asked me to thank everyone for chanting on his behalf. "Where is your brother?" he inquired. I told him with my thought that my brother had to care for his little daughters.

I could not stop crying throughout our communication. He comforted me gently, "Don't worry. All is well." Then he said, "I must go to your mom now."

My vision instantly opened to the hospital waiting area where my mother was lying down on a couch, overcome with grief. My dad's spirit lay down and wrapped itself around her body. He comforted her for some time before coming back to his hospital room. Instead of a gray-haired, frail, and thin old man, my dad now looked like a thirty-something young man with thick dark hair and strong broad shoulders. He asked me to say "thank you" to my mom for taking such good care of him through the years of their long marriage.

After his passing, my dad came back and visited my mom several times on specific dates, in accordance with Chinese beliefs. My mother stated that even though her body was asleep during these visits, her mind was awake and clear. She described the vivid scenes of my dad's visits and the conversations between them.

My mom was perplexed when my dad appeared once with a woman by his side. My mom had thought that, with my dad's faithful personality, there could not be "another woman". "Who is that Korean woman on your side?" my mom asked, seeing that lady's Korean costume. My dad was silent.

I wondered if my dad was showing my mom that he had a Heavenly mate. Maybe he thought it was beyond my mom's earthly concepts to understand about Heavenly mates even if he tried to explain. His Heavenly mate might have gone through her earthly experience in Korea, just as my dad had completed his with us. Or, maybe she just preferred that particular style of costume. Nonetheless, my mom was comforted that my dad had promised again to come for her when it was her time to join him after her crossover.

My mom confided in me several times that she had been skeptical about the existence of life after death. However, all that changed after her encounters with my dad's spirit. She no longer could deny that life continues even without the physical body. And she no longer had any fear of death.

My father also showed up in my sister's dreams, bringing her lots of good food. Symbolically, my dad was encouraging my sister to eat more for the sake of her health, as she ate very little.

One night, my brother was asleep on the floor next to the parts of a bedframe leaning against the wall, waiting to be assembled. My dad tickled my brother's feet until he woke up and shifted his position just before the heavy headboard fell over. But for my dad, my brother would have sustained a serious head injury. My brother talked about seeing my dad in 2020; he had stayed with my brother the entire time during the critical procedure for his lymphoma cancer treatment.

I had a dream three days before my dad's passing. He appeared to me that night, smiling as he poured out Chinese gold coins from three front pockets of a traditional Chinese outfit that I had never seen him wear before. My mom and sister told me that it was a custom to leave what translates to "hand's tip money" at the end of one's life. My dad knew I had been concerned about my finances. In fact, I take advantage of my dad's benevolence in the next dimension just as I had in the earthly one. We had often laughed together when my requests were too demanding or impossible to fulfill.

Pain in Love

Due to the travel restrictions imposed during COVID-19 in 2020, I was not able to visit my mom in Taiwan as regularly as in previous years, especially without citizenship or an updated Taiwanese passport. My brother and sister as well as my friends urged me not to risk contracting the virus by traveling to Taiwan, in view of my age and health conditions and the lack of medical coverage there. My heart was in turmoil. I was concerned about my mom's worsening health, but I did not want to burden my sister and brother with responsibility for my food and lodging. They were extremely exhausted from caring for my mother before and during her stay at the hospital, especially my brother, who was quite weak from his ongoing cancer treatments.

Seeing how desperate I was to get to Taiwan, my brother managed to procure me a special entry permit on June 15th. I immediately purchased a PPE for my trip. However, the flights between Taiwan and the United States were limited to once a week. The earliest flight I might be able to book was on June 22nd. With the mandatory fourteen-day quarantine, it would be July 7th before I could see my mom in person. On June 30th, I was still checking to see if I could secure a seat on a flight to Taiwan. After an intense struggle, I knew it would be wise to consider what my mom would have wanted me to do under the circumstances. Being a thoughtful and loving mom, she certainly would not want me to add more stress on my sister and brother. With painful resolve, I apologized to my mom that evening on the phone and let her know that I would visit her when the virus situation lightened up a bit. (My brother later told me they were relieved to hear I was not coming.) At 7:25 the next morning, July 1st, 2020, my sister informed me that our mom's heart and breathing had simply stopped. My mom had decided to exit her aging body, with its constant pains and limited mobility, after our conversation.

The grief and devastation I felt at my mom's passing was inexpressible. My anguish gushed ceaselessly from the gaping hole in my heart throughout the day. Amazingly, as soon as I awoke the next morning, the unmistakable energy of love softly and filled every space of my bedroom and touched every cell of my body. In fact, the word "love" was inadequate to describe this exquisite, gentle, caressing, wholesome, and beyond beautiful presence. A deep sense of peace accompanied me everywhere as I proceeded with my day. My mom had come and spent the day with me! Surprisingly, my grandma also made her presence known to me on July 3 to let me know that my mom, my dad, and she had met, and all was well. As a child I was quite close to my grandma, who had passed away over forty years ago. But I hadn't thought of her for many years.

Several days later, my mom appeared to me in a dream. At first, she was lying comfortably in my dad's arms, wearing a soft floral dress in a style that I did not recognize immediately, since it was not my mom's usual attire, nor was it commonly seen in my daily life. All of a sudden, she jumped up and hopped all around in a frenzy, telling me that it was very hot. She then showed me many burnt patches on her face and body. My sister-in-law later confirmed with me that my mom was wearing the traditional Chinese "qipao" dress with floral print worn for her cremation. My mom and I had enjoyed joking with each other, often laughing until tears ran down our cheeks in our earthly exchanges.

Maybe she was confirming to me what has been proven medically—that our physical body does not die immediately and completely. Our physical functions shut down organ by organ, cell by cell, while our consciousness gradually exits out of this sacred earthly instrument. The tedious but important and meaningful process is similar to the process of entering our physical body.

For weeks after her passing, I would automatically reach for my phone to connect with my mom at our regular time each day. But sadly, my best friend, with whom I had confided my secrets and shared my joy or sorrow, was silent at the other end. This sage, who had accepted and loved me unconditionally, despite all my faults and the hurts I had brought her, was forever gone from this world. Our joyous laughter, nonsense chattering, and deep sharing echoed in my mind. No longer could I take a picture of my mom doing her favorite Hawaiian *shaka* gesture with her hands. Nor could I be the sulking little girl seeking comfort from her. The special place in my arms for my mom was now empty and cold. I could not stop my tears . . .

During many moments of my grieving, a warm current of tender love would ever so gently infuse my whole being. The healing power of love would elevate me to the state of "all is well." I felt calm, content, safe, and indistinguishable from the love itself. I wished to stay in the comforting cradle of my mom's love forever. But every thought of my mom sliced my heart into pieces. I could not help but call to her for comfort— *Mom, Mom, Mom . . .*

An impression from my mom softly announced the following: *The degree of pain is not equivalent to the intensity of love, nor can distance separate the love we share . . .*

I knew that my mom was trying to soothe my grief. I can certainly feel the presence of my mom and dad and connect with their spirit any time. I am very happy that my mom no longer suffers physically, and I am proud of her great accomplishments on Earth. Nevertheless, I couldn't help but beg to her:

Please stay a bit longer and let me tell you again how thankful to you I am for giving me life. Thank you for walking by my side so patiently during my earthly journey. Please, beloved wonderful Mom, don't take away my most beautiful Gift of Love—You! My heart just cannot stop yearning for you . . . I miss you so much and I Love You!!

All Is Well

Due to the COVID-19 restrictions, our family members living in the United States were not able to attend my mom's memorial service held in Taiwan in July 2020. So, we decided that each of us would say a few words and provide some personal photos with mom/grandma for a joint video to be shown at the memorial service. This video turned out to be very beautiful and heartwarming. However, I had a shock when I viewed my daughter's contribution.

One of the photos in her video piece was a selfie she had taken during our visit with my mom in 2006. (That trip was right before she came to live with me for a couple of years.) At her request, all three of us had lain down with our eyes closed, as if resting peacefully together; she was in between her grandmother and me. She had told us this photo portrayed the love and peace shared between mothers and daughters. She had had this selfie printed on a computer mouse pad and presented it to me as my Mother's Day gift the next year. In the video version, not only had she cut me out of the picture, but she had put photos of my sister and my mom right after it—as if to say that they were her "real" mothers. My sister would be attending the service, so I saw no need for her photo to be in this video. My daughter had hundreds of photos taken with her grandmother to choose from. But she picked this particular one. Her message could not have been clearer.

Feeling intensely hurt, I interpreted my daughter's behavior as a vindictive declaration against me. Fuming with a kind of anger that I had never felt toward her in her entire life, my mind screamed: *How could her heart be so cold to my repeated humble apologies and efforts of love? How could she cast the stones of judgment at me when she also has weaknesses? Most of all, how could she take advantage of my mom's memorial service to disrespect the mother who had birthed and cared for her the best she could, and dishonor her grandma who had always emphasized family unity and gratitude?*

My emotional steam gradually evaporated from this egoic outburst, and my heart had softened by the next day. In a state of calmness and love, my being began merging with my daughter in the consciousness of loving Oneness. A vision appeared. I was shocked to see blood covering my outstretched but empty hands; my little baby girl was no longer there to hold. The blood trailed back to my broken heart. Then, I saw tears streaming down my face as I felt my daughter's anguish, fear, and lack—and especially her pain from feeling deserted by her birth mother; now her beloved grandma was gone, too.

Another vivid dream came later. I was alone in a dark room and heard my daughter's cries of sadness and helplessness. I looked all over for her frantically. I screamed her name at the top of my lungs and asked repeatedly, "Where are you? Where are you? Mommy is here! Mommy is here!" I was more panicked and frightened with each passing second of not finding her. When I went outside the room, I saw a man carrying my now unconscious daughter in his arms toward a car. He threatened me by holding a blade against my daughter's throat. Somehow I was able to make him drop my daughter on the ground as I fought him with all my might, but I could not defeat him and was covered in blood from my injuries. As he started driving away with my daughter, I threw myself against the windshield in desperation. Trying to break the windshield, I used all of my body, pounding and stomping forcefully. Suddenly, the horrific sight of crushed glass and gushing blood from my limbs disappeared. It was 3:00 a.m., the night after Mother's Day in 2021. I stayed awake the rest of the night, shaken with loss and devastation.

The vision and the dream about my daughter somehow shocked my consciousness into seeing that I had judged her dad and other people, situations, and events in a way that was like what she had done to me and others in her life. When I looked at the extensive trauma that not understanding our ego can cause in our relationships with one another, I shivered. I finally realized that the essence of ego is the opposite of love — *the lack of love*. When the intelligence of our heart is weakened by the lack of love, we often cannot recognize the significance of someone until that person had gone from our life. Nor can we value something until we have experienced its loss. The lack of love for ourselves and others prevents us from seeing our own and others' true beauty, worth, and perfection. Most of all, the ego, instead of sharing abundance as "you *and* me," divides us into "you *or* me" to compete in the world. By working through the layers of the ego, experiencing, and learning from its sacred darkness, we can reveal the light of our truth.

Both darkness and light are necessary for "life" to be "alive." They have the same purpose and dedication that not only lead us to rediscover and reclaim our true self on Earth, but also enrich our divine truth with the wisdom harvested from our earthly experiences. Their sacred partnership transcends and frees us to true love.

I was relieved to have come to this understanding and to have found peace with my relationship with my daughter and with the people closest to me in my life. I respect however my daughter and others choose to shine their light. Ultimately, all is valid, valuable, and loved unconditionally by the supreme Universe.

A smile lights up my face whenever I look at my daughter's photos hanging on my walls or displayed in frames in my home. If only I could cradle her beautiful essence in my arms and whisper these words tenderly to her:

My precious, thank you for being my "soul duster" to clean up my egoic-self for my true self. I am ready to listen and snuggle up to your beautiful divinity now. Let's create and appreciate the magic of life together. Let's celebrate our mother-daughter-friend moments. I am so proud of how you live your life. Be happy! I love you!

6

The Smile of the Universe

Omni-Dynamic Energy

A few months after I had witnessed the birth of Aesina, the Heavenly Parents showed me a scene in which millions of light sparks exploded out of their extended arms. Somehow, I just knew they were creating their spirit children. But I was puzzled. *How could they birth millions of spirit children simultaneously? Did they create other forms and matter with their thoughts and the gesture of their arms, too?* My limited human intellect could not begin to fathom the creative power of the infinite Universe. It seemed that not only could our Heavenly Parents extract endless energy from the Universe for their own endeavors, but that everything in the Universe is created with this same energy. Everything is sustained by and thrives on it. I call it the "omni-dynamic" energy.

Another marvel I witnessed about the omnipotent, omnipresent, and omniscient Heavenly Parents was the equal respect they showed for seemingly insignificant beings and forms. They gifted very spirit being with the divine consciousness of perfect love, creative power, and superior intelligence. Every spirit is composed of wholesome energies, including but not limited to the energies of talents, character, propensities, and both male and female energies. For the purpose of gaining experience, learning, and growing, the spirit can decide how much and in what way this energy will be expressed through the role it takes on during its earthly excursion.

The Heavenly Parents ask the spirit's preferences before creating its existence, from the tiniest details of its attributes, abilities, and predisposition. Moreover, the spirit is fully informed of its mission, responsibilities, and the outcome of its choices. Each spirit being can enjoy free will and is encouraged to balance, harmonize, remediate, or replace anew the effects of its choices.

Heavenly Spa

One day, I felt absolutely discouraged after dealing with a difficult client who I had trusted as my friend. When I got home from that session, I cried my heart out, crushed by his insolence and insults about my professional ability. To calm myself, I entered a vision that led me to a font shaped like a deep well and filled with a soft white cloud-like energy. I saw myself submerge my body in this "Heavenly Spa." I did not suffocate like a physical body would while entirely under water since this was my spirit body.

That was the first time I had seen my spirit body without a robe on. As soon as I wondered what Michael's spirit body looked like, I saw him standing just a few steps away from the font. My thought upon seeing our naked spirit bodies was, *They are so plain.* There were no features to distinguish the male from the female spirit body since reproductive organs were not necessary. Also, the spirit bodies had no specific internal parts, such as the lungs or digestive organs that an earthly body needs to survive.

I felt quite refreshed when I stepped out. All my frustration and resentment had completely disappeared. For the next few days, I often sang joyfully, and a smile was pasted on my face. Since that incident, I have not shed any more tears over business-related matters, regardless of how unreasonable certain clients can be.

***

There was a time when I suffered from constant pain throughout my body, likely a precursor to the fibromyalgia that I would eventually have for the rest of my life. One day, I heard a spiritual prompting to get in my car and drive to a green pasture that I had never visited before. I was led to lie down on a peaceful grassy spot beside a small stream that flowed into the bay. Miraculously, I could feel the physical pain that had lasted for several months dissipate, little by little, out of my body as it touched Mother Earth. I discovered that my friends' physical pain could also be relieved by this "earthly spa" when I took them there to receive the healing energy from Mother Earth.

Plant Talk

I enjoy regularly hiking in nature. I always offer my gratitude to nature's majestic beauty and healing energy. One day in a vision, I asked some plants how their life had been. Nature's changes on Earth through the eons immediately appeared: I saw the formation of hills and mountains, the courses of the rivers and oceans, the shifting of the ground and the composition of the soil, and the various growth stages of the plant life.

I was amazed at the infinite intelligence of everything in nature. Being in tune with the energy of Mother Earth, the animals, plants, and all the other inhabitants in nature can sense the onset of drought, fire, or floods before humans can. The plants demonstrated to me how they could shrink the size of their exposed surfaces and retract every bit of the water and nutrients from each vein of the leaves and branches down into the roots before and during drought or fire. Therefore, there would be a storage of supplies and water to sustain the new growth when the ground was ready.

They also let me see how they manage during a flood. They would absorb beneficial nutrients while filtering out excess toxins through their leaves, branches, and roots. Afterward, they would shut off their "valves" from all their surface areas to prevent excess water from damaging their roots. Renewal was thus achieved, and new life created.

Despite the appearance of wilting or decay, I saw that their roots were alive and interacting with creatures underground, the ants, beetles, worms, reptiles, etc. They jokingly told me that they were not just "party animals," but that they respected and honored the support system that sustained them. While receiving sustenance from Mother Earth, they reciprocated by providing food, shelter, and playgrounds for humans and other living things.

The plants emphasized that everything in nature has feelings and sensitivities just like humans or even more. They serve us with pure love and wish for humans to show them respect too, as such reverence ultimately benefits all of us. What a sight I had witnessed! Their parting words to me were these: "Nothing is what it seems."

The Game of Light

There is a pillar of light located near the Heavenly Spa in my Heavenly home that Michael and I share. It is shaped like a cone that reaches up to a boundless height and consists of billions of tiny brilliant white and gold sparkles. I often stepped inside this pillar of light whenever my energy needed rejuvenation. My body would float midair inside this cone of light, as if weightless. Besides getting a warm feeling, every inch of my skin would tingle, and my physical body would sometimes perspire inside this glorious light. My spirit would be uplifted, and my physical body felt energized afterward. I often saw the Heavenly Parents standing on the side, watching me. They sometimes infused their energy into this pillar of light, as if pouring flower nectar into the feeder of an insatiable hummingbird.

***

Sometimes, a light of considerable magnitude would hit me with a big bang while I was in bed. It felt as if my room had been struck by a meteoroid or thunderbolt. My body would jerk with convulsions from the force. At other times, a dot of brilliant golden light would hang over my forehead like a light bulb. It was a small dot of light, but it seemed to project a million-volt force. I had to jokingly ask whoever and whatever was keeping this "loving post" over me to take a break so that I could sleep.

***

One day, some years before my parents' passing, they called me from Hawaii and told me about an interesting phenomenon. At around 4:45 that morning, both had been awakened by a bright light that filled their bedroom entirely. They got up and checked every other room in the house to see if the lights were on. However, there was only darkness in the other parts of the house, as dark as the sky outside, and no light switches had been turned on. The light in their bedroom lasted a few more minutes before it disappeared.

***

I called my mom almost every day while she was still on Earth. It was surprising to find her in despair one morning, as she was always so cheerful. She told me that she could not bear the thought of losing the little bit of eyesight she had left since her accident from a fall years ago.

I was very concerned and asked, "What's the matter? Why are you having such thoughts?"

"I have been seeing a blue color since yesterday. I have called my optometrist for a checkup later this afternoon," she replied with dismay.

Suddenly, something hit me. Two days earlier, instead of the white light that I usually sent to her and others for joy and love, I was inspired to send her the blue light of healing. She later confirmed that her optometrist had found no further regression or anything wrong with her vision.

The Heavenly Atrium

Holly is very trusting and open to receiving messages and guidance from the spiritual realm. She expressed the need for help as she was working on her part of this book. A divine gift indeed arrived! At one of our spiritual administrations at her home in 2015, I saw an atrium in my vision that opened to the spiritual realm in the place where she usually did her writing.

~ 125 ~

I saw brilliant lights pouring into this "Heavenly Atrium" from the ceiling. I told her that by standing in this tube of light, she would be energized by the pure energy and receive inspiration to assist her with writing.

Surprisingly, this atrium was closed when I visited her again after she had returned from a trip overseas. I figured that it might have been necessary to close the passageway so as not to attract undesirable earthly energies. I decided to shoot piercing white light upward through the ceiling with my thoughts; but the passageway did not open as easily as I had expected. I asked Archangel Michael and all those in Heaven to help.

To my amazement, I saw with my spirit eyes something like a steel block, at least twelve inches thick, near the ceiling. There were several sheets of energy grids on top of the block, with bars of golden light crossing over each other. Much like drilling through a heavy metal partition, I pushed hard skyward from underneath with my white light and the beings in the spiritual realm penetrated the golden sheets by pushing downward with their powerful energies. By sandwiching the thick metal block with powerful light from beneath and above, at last we were able to open the atrium again.

I had little knowledge about the different dimensions or energy fields. However, I felt that I had probably witnessed what those who go through a Near Death Experience (NDE) describe about crossing over from Earth to Heaven. The thick steel-like barricade in my vision resembles the dark tunnel before someone reaches the light at the end. The various sheets of light perhaps signify different dimensions. The existence of the different dimensions might have a special purpose to assist the returning spirits to recognize and experience different sensations, and thus ease them into the spiritual realm.

Humanly Divine

One time in a vision, I saw Aesina draped in the veil that Michael had gifted her in 2007. Serenity and loveliness filled the air as Aesina walked gracefully out to the garden, with the long veil, made of stars, moons, and ocean, trailing softly behind her. She had turned her head to gaze steadily at me as she walked. I felt a strong sense of connection with Aesina (as me), even though my mind still couldn't quite accept myself as Aesina. She seemed to be conveying something to me through the laser-like yet gentle rays of light from her dark eyes. And then I saw the early stage of my earthly life open up.

Aesina was cuddling me as a newborn baby; I was crying and sucking my thumb for comfort, frightened by the unknown new life on Earth. She held me when I woke up crying from having to leave the security and perfect love in Heaven. She cleared my eyes to enable me to see that I was never a helpless victim of life but a courageous heroine of the earthly academy. She nudged me to listen to my inner guidance and utilize the power of knowledge to heal myself and others, physically, emotionally, and spiritually.

She told me that vulnerability is a "sacred pride" that summons courage and honesty to meet our sufferings such as our fear, pain, disappointment, frustration, and confusion. Vulnerability is an expression of self-love. It embodies the divine trust that invites absolute gratitude into our being, without any expectation of result. Vulnerability empowers us to live in integrity, and to acknowledge our human limitations. It supports the desire to learn and improve, the willingness to unbridle our potential, and the humility and gratitude to accept support. In order to fortify this "sacred pride" during our earthly experiences in the world of duality, paradox, and polarity, it is necessary to apply wisdom. Therefore, we need to consider all the circumstances, including the people, and matters involved, to best demonstrate our love.

Aesina would gently alert me whenever I was entertaining ego. On the other hand, she would jolt me sharply away from physical harm. Aesina was integrating her divine essence into my human life. She is my higher consciousness and my true self.

It felt like hours had passed during that communion with Aesina, but seconds later, she began to gather up the millions of pieces of "me." Each "me" was created from my thoughts, desires, emotions, and actions. An astonishingly beautiful bouquet of flowers of countless unnamable varieties, in a myriad of colors, soon filled her arms. These flowers emitted delightful fragrances and vivid lights to communicate their impressions of understanding, with brilliant intelligence and great love. They praised the ingeniousness of my fear and ego, as they are a necessary evil to help us learn about and ascertain the "divine bliss." This joy is a Heavenly elixir filled with the power of loving Oneness and infinite peace. It is the Miracle of Love that heals our suffering and enables human greatness. The flowers danced exuberantly whenever my heart and my mind worked together to harmonize my inner and outer worlds. Their songs became more exquisite, and their colors deepened into ever subtler shades, when my acts and thoughts were in alignment with truth and expanded my knowledge. In my stillness, each petal whispered to me in the thunderous silence of serenity. My heartbeat echoed the rhythm of the eternal breath.

Aesina then buried her head in this bouquet and breathed in deeply, as if feasting upon its energy. To my astonishment, Aesina and the bouquet began to expand outward. Their outline became a blur, and she was no longer identifiable as she merged into a supreme perfection and wholeness. This pure Heavenly consciousness appeared in my mind's eye as an infinite void or space of nothingness. And yet contained within it were lively expressions of individual uniqueness.

When Oneness expresses its divine intelligence, beauty, and joy through us we experience this pure love with all our senses—and more! This heavenly bliss is beyond explanation. Colors and sounds vibrate the taste and fragrance of love. Every form in existence is alive with this magnificent creative power.

All in a Day's Work

The Heavenly Father came to me a few days later. I was thrilled to see him and inquired about the purpose of his visit. He chuckled in that familiar way I loved so much, winked at me, and gave me a mysterious look without answering my question.

To my great delight, within an instant, the Heavenly Father and I were in the presence of the Heavenly Mother. I saw the Heavenly Mother swiftly throw her right arm in front of her and point. Countless lights with varying degrees of intensity shot out of her fingers into the dark canvas of space. Some of the lights flew like lightning bolts, long and powerful; others were tiny sparkles, as soft and delicate as feathers. These lights were accompanied by sounds, colors, melodies, fragrances, and various forms or shapes. It seemed that the Heavenly Mother was generating and directing the energy that formulated the thoughts, feelings, consciousness, and unconsciousness of all beings, as well as their behavior. She was also controlling the frequency of energetic vibrations to create the inspiration, information, motivation, emotions, and desires that resonate with the rhythm of life. Under her direction, the cosmos was alive with expressive dances in accordance with the purposes of the creations. I realized that the Heavenly Mother was attending to the needs of all beings and supervising everything that was happening in the Universe.

It was impossible to see all the specifics playing out on the surface or grasp the complete picture, as it was vast and extended beyond my view. However, a familiar "knowing" rushed through me, swift as one of those lights shooting out of the Heavenly Mother's fingers. My being could identify the details of her masterpiece as well as embrace the whole with clarity and appreciation. I immediately understood the purpose of each individual light by its specific formation. I could also merge with and reflect the expression of each light. Moreover, I witnessed the works of energy from the smallest atomic particle to the grandest scale of constituents, from physically perceivable matter to the indiscernible sensed through energy. I could also see the correlations between them and understood exactly why they are the way that they are. To my further amazement, pure love was in everything, even in the most unlikely places, and had functions that my human mind would not have believed or comprehended. Where there is love, there is light—and vice versa. They sustain each other and transform into each other.

With the assistance of pure love and divine intelligence, I could comprehend the purpose of each dimension and the effect of its interaction with the other dimensions. All dimensions are connected with each other and work together as one indivisible unit for the grand purpose of the Universe. I could also communicate with many other forms of living beings and participate in their lives through the coordination and alignment of energy. Consequently, I was empowered to cherish the value and beauty of every existence. Taking part in every occurrence, I also recognized myself as an indispensable co-contributor to the *Life* of the Universe, where everyone and everything is part of the whole fabric.

What's more, I saw the profound mechanisms to human consciousness, divine consciousness, and absolute consciousness (in which human and divine consciousness are merged as One). I understood the polarity between ego and spirituality. It is through the coordination of darkness and light, separation and unity, finite and infinite that our life is enriched and the universal truth revealed to us. Also unveiled to me was the significance of the free will that empowers our creative genius to fly and co-pilot the causal effects. The more I observed the interplay of these innumerable facets that influence every being and form in this grand Universe, material and non-material, the more humbled I became.

Afterward, I could not remember the details or retrieve the capacities I had while with the Heavenly Parents in that vision. However, "the eternal truth of life" had powerfully wedged itself into my very core. I felt light, refreshed, and rejuvenated. My being flew with joy into the unlimited heights for several days.

The Smile of the Universe

A couple of years after viewing the Heavenly Parents' creation of their spirit children, I became daring and questioned how the Heavenly Parents themselves had come into existence. I did not know who to ask or where to go to get the honest answer. In frustration, I screamed my question into space. Startled, I heard a breathing sound fill up the space and a very solemn and weighty voice echoed in the infinite void:

The Mother God is my divine in form. She has created her Heavenly mate, your Heavenly Father, to assist her in the functions of the Universe.

As if knowing I would be stunned and resist accepting this message, the Universe repeated this declaration several times over the next year and a half.

Was this a delusion? I wondered. Why would "The Master of All" care enough to answer the request of insignificant me? Seek and ye shall find? Also, how could I reconcile this with the traditional "beginning" story of my beloved Heavenly Father. It contradicted the beliefs of the patriarchal world. I was dumbfounded. To appease my logical mind, I tried to equate the creative capacity of the Mother God with that of Mother Earth, as both are the source and life-givers of all there IS. I also attributed to them the energy of feminine nature (not necessarily related to female gender), that is heart- and soul-centered wisdom, healing, and softness with strength. Many anthropologists believe that a matriarchal system, with nurturing traits, existed from the time of the Gynocritic Age, around two million years ago, up to 3,000 BCE; after which it was replaced by the patriarchal system with traits of dominance and control. Additionally, many scholars and archeologists have discovered that the feminine energy was honored before the patriarchy got rid of the images and sacred literature about the feminine dimension of the divine, in order to exert their control and power around 621 BCE. Over the ages, the suppression and repression of the female divinity has altered our personal human connection with the Universe.

Unexpectedly, as I was writing this part of my story, the Universe "reached out" to answer me. Somehow, I *just knew* it was *IT*. Surprised by this, I asked, "What's up?"

The Universe smiled. Immediately, my being was wrapped entirely and melted completely into its Beingness. I was indistinguishable from *IT*. Nevertheless, as the smallest possible particle of light in the silent stillness of *IT*s seeming Void and Nothingness, I had an awareness that could witness *IT* as the substance of all life, forms, and dynamics. I could understand the value of my existence and experiences. Amazingly, I also felt super smart and powerful as a part of the whole of the Universe. Contained within *IT*s inestimably brilliant light, pure love filled me with absolute gratitude and beautified my being. Resonating to the music of the Universe, I came "home" to the ineffable Bliss of Loving Oneness!

Suddenly, the scene changed. Lying in front of me in a very bright space was a clown costume, sewn together with patches of cloth in various shapes and assorted colorful prints. My attention was drawn to shards of mirrored glass piercing the cloth all over the costume. *Ouch!* was my initial thought. *Why a clown costume? What does it mean?* The Universe sure enjoys tickling our mind and senses with mystery, intrigue, and humor.

Leaving me to work out this perplexity, the Universe gently brought me back to my earthly reality. The tears that had welled up in my heart from the first moment of my rendezvous with the Universe trickled down my face; it felt as if my most dearly beloved had departed from me. How I wanted to remain eternally in the *absolute grace and goodness* that had filled me with such exaltation. I had felt totally understood, accepted, respected, valued, and loved unconditionally. I felt whole, free, and happy!

To each his or her own. We all choose different experiences in life. And different minds can have vastly different interpretations. As I see it now, the clown costume in my simple vision represents the ego roles that we take on during our earthly journey. Our ego can lure our mind into creative and fun adventures, or it can subject us to painful challenges. I see the sharp piercing glass on the clown suit as a symbol of the afflictions that can stimulate our spiritual awakening. Crises often open up new possibilities, and the deepest suffering can catalyze the greatest growth. It's important to know that we are free to take off this "clown costume" whenever we desire.

This vision enabled me to better understand the title I was given for this book in my 2007 vision: "The Loving Connection." The Universe is a living energy field of light with supreme consciousness that emits pure love and infinite intelligence. Every existence is sourced from the same powerful energy, the light in the Universe. Yet every existence has a different density and vibrational frequency, and each illuminates its own intensity of light. Energy is love and serves love. Thus, existence serves and supports each creation through this divine bond of love. In the state of pure consciousness, all beings, forms, and formless energies desire to support each other through this common bond of love. All of this joyfully breathes, dances, sings, and resonates together in the eternal *Life* of the Universe.

How grateful I am to know we are here on Earth as embodiments of the Universe, fellow spirits in earthly bodies expanding our souls through human experiences. Each one of us came to Earth with different strengths and weaknesses to seed new ideas and new ways of being. Our soul contracts can refine each other's soulful intentions and revivify the energy of the Universe. We are our own master to direct how we resonate with our divine beingness while traversing the rainbow of the Universe. With compassion and gratitude, we can turn ugly lumps of soot into gorgeous diamonds for one another—and stun the Universe with our beauty.

Every one of us is an angel of light and love. Let us keep our porch lights on until every last one of us is safely home.

And now it is time for me to seal this gift of love with a smile.

Part Two
The Story of Holly
(aka Nena)

INTRODUCTION
The Initiation

I was a client of LeAnn Chen over two decades ago, having consulted her about a legal matter. Meeting again at a mutual friend's gathering a couple of years later, we found that we were both intrigued by the mystical. I learned about her clairvoyant abilities, such as being able to see the spirit world and receive messages from the Heavenly realm. She also knew how to perform psychic readings and consult geomancy (feng shui)—all without prior study. LeAnn didn't boast of these abilities, since they came naturally to her.

In May 2007, LeAnn offered to perform an energy healing on me to help improve my frail health. She had recently discovered that she could revitalize dying flowers and plants by transferring energy to them through her thoughts. When we discovered that the energy healings she performed on me brought messages from the spiritual realm, which further benefited my body, mind, and spirit, LeAnn suggested we called these ceremonies "spiritual administrations." The messages in these healing ceremonies were so profound and full of love and truth from the Heavenly Parents that we started recording every one of them in 2012. Some of the information I have shared in my story was taken directly from our transcriptions of these recordings since that time.

During the spiritual administration on September 18, 2012, I was told to write about "Jullian and Little Cutie" for this book, *The Loving Connection*, that LeAnn was inspired to start writing in 2007. Jullian is my Heavenly mate, and Little Cutie is the spiritual nickname that Archangel Michael had lovingly given me. My name in the spirit world is "Nena."

To my shock, I was also instructed to write about body, mind, and spirit for this book during a Spiritual Administration in May 2014. I almost dug a hole in the ground and buried myself in it from embarrassment. I did not feel up to the task, as I was still exploring and learning about spirituality, and I am not a writer either.

Seeing my struggle, the Heavenly spirits offered their support during our Spiritual Administration in January 2015. An energy tube, which we called "the Heavenly atrium," was placed beside the desk where I did my writing to enable me to communicate directly with the spiritual realm. I was told that by standing in this tube of Heavenly light, I would be energized as well as receive inspiration for my writing.

I began to consciously observe my moods and thoughts, and to trust the guidance from my inner wisdom. I diligently learned how to attain inner balance and harmony through my life experiences. Even though the writing was never easy, I was surprised to see how the act of writing about this exciting period of spiritual discovery and self-inquiry deepened my understanding. I am grateful to my family and friends for giving me the opportunities to practice learning about love. They have enabled me to look at others and myself from a new perceptive.

I feel relieved and comforted that I was finally able to complete my part of this book, a mission that I had thought would be impossible to accomplish. I am honored to share love, joy, peace, and gratitude with readers through the stories in this book.

Holly Lin

7

The Enlightenment Ceremony

*I*n May of 2007, LeAnn Chen and I met at my home for my third energy healing. By then, I was personally familiar with her extraordinary psychic abilities, and impressed by the results of my first two healing sessions with her. I told her that I was very honored and willing to be her "guinea pig" during our mutual spiritual exploration.

To show the proper respect for this ceremony held in my bedroom, I reverently poured two cups of water for us, turned off my cellphone, and shut the door to avoid any disturbances. Then I lay down on my bed. LeAnn sat next to me, told me to take deep breaths, and guided me into a tranquil state. My body gradually felt more and more relaxed. As our hearts and minds became still, we sensed our surroundings also becoming still. LeAnn then offered a sincere prayer with words full of love and gratitude. She invited the Heavenly Parents and my family and friends in the spiritual world to join us and share their love and wisdom with us. She expressed to them that we were not only willing to open our hearts and minds to listen to their guidance but also would humbly follow it. She then closed her eyes with concentration, while waiting for instructions from the spiritual realm.

After a moment, she began by saying, "Today is a very special day for an important celebration. Your family and friends in the spirit world, including your deceased father-in-law and your late mother, are all here participating in this event. I can hear beautiful music and singing. I also see many children happily scattering all kinds of colorful flowers. Everyone is rejoicing. All of them feel honored to be able to attend this celebration."

She went on, "I see a ray of white light entering through the crown of your head into your body. Its purpose is to strengthen the weak parts of your body."

I instantly felt a surge of energy, like a warm current gently infusing the cells in my body. It felt particularly warm in my throat, lungs, shoulder, and waist, the weakest areas of my body.

She explained, "Holly, the Heavenly Parents are the ones conducting this enlightenment ceremony. The purpose is to help you open the door to spirituality and the window of wisdom, as well as to assist in your awakening. There is a beam of white light entering through your third eye into your body now."

Immediately, I felt a gush of energy circulating rapidly inside me, as if a lightning bolt had charged every single cell of my body. My back arched up several times from the force of the energy. And yet, the feeling was not uncomfortable at all. My body was wrapped completely in this warm energy. I was immersed in the feeling of being embraced by love, which felt very familiar—like home. The love from the spiritual realm touched my heart so deeply that I was moved to tears.

Next, LeAnn Chen said, "The Heavenly Parents asked me to let you know that you can pray and ask for guidance from them and from the angels when you cannot make a decision. Inspiration will come to you when your heart is still. LeAnn Chen will be your mentor. You will have a shared mission."

At the conclusion of the ceremony, my deceased father-in-law and my late mother expressed their love and gave me blessings through LeAnn. I thanked them for participating in this wonderful sacred ceremony with me. My heart was filled with great respect for them. I also felt tremendous gratitude for the spiritual realm.

After the ceremony, LeAnn and I exclaimed in unison, "We have a shared mission!" However, we did not yet understand the meaning of this mission.

LeAnn was very modest and said, "I feel incompetent and dare not be your mentor." She did not know of her spiritual identity as "Aesina" at the time.

An impressive thing happened to those two cups of water that I had poured for us before the ceremony. We were both amazed when we tasted the water. It was like liquid manna, a sweet Heavenly nectar. *How did this water become so sweet and flavorful?* I wondered. Interestingly, I also noticed that a warm electrical current was still running throughout my body.

After the enlightenment ceremony, we went to a restaurant where a live jazz band was playing outside in the square. Our hearts were filled with joy, and we danced happily with the others to the lively music. While dining together, LeAnn told me that my late mother had been with me all that time. She described what she saw when she looked at my mother, whom LeAnn had never seen before. My mother had been gone from this world for two years. I believed it was my mother she described, because LeAnn saw her wearing her favorite outfits during her lifetime.

LeAnn repeated a word that sounded like *"han."* I suddenly remembered that "Han" was what my parents had called me. My mother was using this method to prove her presence. She wanted me to know that her love was always with me.

That same evening, I offered some of the "Heavenly nectar" from the healing ceremony to my husband, while sharing the details about the water with excitement. My husband listened patiently with an incredulous expression but agreed to taste it. "This water tastes like nothing special," he said.

I drank a mouthful of it myself and agreed with his opinion. The sweet-tasting water had been restored to its original state. It occurred to me at that moment that there must be a time limit for the effects of certain energy.

Lying in bed that night, I felt a warm and tingling sensation all over my body. I soon fell asleep, but when I awoke at 3:00 a.m., the same warm and tender energy was circulating in my body. As long as I stayed relaxed, this energy kept flowing through me in a rhythmic movement. It lasted a whole hour, after which my body was completely drenched with sweat.

***

This particular healing experience had a stunning impact on me. I began to learn about spirituality with an open mind. I am now certain about the existence of the spiritual world—that is, I believe that Heaven is for real. I had grown up in a family that identified with Buddhism, as did many in Taiwan. The only contact I had with Christianity was in the seventh grade when I attended a Christian school. When I married my husband at twenty years old, I continued to follow Buddhist beliefs and customs, as he and his family were devout Buddhists. So, although I did not understand the unknown realm, I was always aware that an unseen world existed.

After this enlightenment ceremony, I asked LeAnn to provide energy healing on a regular basis. And that is how our mission together as a spiritual team began. During the Spiritual Administration she had performed, she not only opened portals to the spirit world to receive healing energy, but she also received messages for both of us from the beyond.

8

Jullian and Little Cutie

Meeting Jullian

*I*n October of 2007, the wildfires had been raging and spreading rapidly for several days in the east part of the city due to the extreme drought conditions. More than one thousand homes were reported to have been destroyed in the fire. Everyone was on high alert and closely followed the news broadcasts for an announcement of a mandatory evacuation should the wind change directions.

Before leaving for work one morning, my husband advised me earnestly:

"Unless necessary, please don't go outdoors. There is too much ash polluting the air and covering the neighborhoods."

I looked out the window and saw that the sky was completely covered with a murky dark grey cloud. Suddenly, I felt like calling Aesina to ask her if the sky in her area looked the same. (After LeAnn learned her spiritual name in July 2007, I began to call her "Aesina.") To my surprise, she informed me that when she looked out her windows, the sky was a clear blue. In disbelief, I asked again. Her answer was still the same: "The sky is a clear blue!" I just could not put my curiosity to rest, so I decided to drive over there immediately and see for myself.

On my way to Aesina's house, everywhere I looked, ashes from the forest fire lay like a thick gray blanket over everything. Nevertheless, an amazing sight greeted me soon after I exited the freeway to her house. In the distance, I saw that a portion of the sky above Aesina's neighborhood was a clear blue. The contrast was extreme when comparing it with the area outside her neighborhood.

After expressing my initial amazement upon arriving at Aesina's home, I told her that my heart was troubled from one of the chapters I had read in a book about soulmates. Knowing that Aesina had the power to instantly communicate with the spiritual realm, my intense curiosity made me blurt out this question: "Do I have a soulmate in the spirit world?"

"Yes," she said. "But they are called Heavenly mates there. Like Archangel Michael is for me. When the Heavenly Father and the Heavenly Mother created us, they also created our Heavenly mates according to the free will of each spirit and his or her personality and individual needs. Some spirits chose to be single."

Without missing a beat, Aesina told me, "Your Heavenly mate's name is 'Jullian.' He is a biologist who loves nature and relishes blending into it. He is a young spirit with a vivacious personality; very cheerful, simple, and peaceful. He is very concerned about you, so he often visits you while you are asleep."

My chest was filled with strong feelings when Aesina passed along the next piece of information; it was the first communication Jullian sent me: *I love you very much!*

Burning with curiosity, I continued to ask, "What is my name in the spirit world?"

Aesina answered, "In the spirit world, your name is *Nena*. You were very cute and quite mischievous. You liked to joke and preferred lacy clothing. You were cared for, guided, and grew up in the household of Archangels Michael and Aesina. Archangel Michael took care of you like his own beloved daughter. He even lovingly gave you a nickname, *Little Cutie*."

Even though I had faith in Aesina's spiritual power, I maintained my skepticism about the unknown world.

When Aesina and I went to a restaurant that evening, something strange happened to me, unlike anything I had experienced. Different parts of my face felt itchy. This itchiness was deep under the skin. I also felt a tickling sensation, as if a hair had fallen on my face. I tried to brush it away, but my effort was in vain. I suddenly realized that Jullian was attempting to communicate with me. It was a playful way for him to say *hello* and prove his existence to me.

Thereafter, I had a similar experience several evenings in a row when I sat down to watch television. I not only felt a slight numbness and itchiness on my face but also felt intense itchiness in my ears, as if being tickled by a feather. Even more remarkable were the sensations when I lay down on my bed every night, ready to sleep. As soon as I had relaxed, it felt as if my body was moving. In fact, my body was not really moving; it was feeling the sensation of incoming energy melting into it. My chest began to fill with warmth, while warmth was also rising from my abdominal area. My instincts told me that Jullian was hugging me. So, I used my thought to bid him good night.

That same feeling returned so many times after the first experience that I decided to test to see if I was hallucinating. I closed my eyes and reached out my hands to feel the air around me. I felt an energy current above my body, as well as numbness and heaviness in my palms and my fingers—as if I were touching a magnetic field. I was stunned. I had never experienced anything like this before in my life. These feelings were so real in my everyday life that I could not help but believe that a spirit was living with me. Consequently, I started learning to communicate with Jullian through my thoughts.

My Silent Partner

At the spiritual administration in September 2012, the Heavenly Parents asked me to write about my experiences with Jullian, my Heavenly mate. Jullian requires Aesina's help to communicate with me as I cannot see or hear him. However, I can feel warm energy when he is with me. I wondered, *Why is Jullian acting as a silent partner to me? What is the significance?*

I learned from Aesina that Jullian had been to the Earth a long time ago, even before the creation of life on Earth. With the Heavenly Parents' permission and blessing, he had chosen to experience the earthly life with me when my spiritual understanding had reached a certain maturity. He was concerned that I would reject him because of disbelief if he appeared too soon in my life.

Jullian and I exist in different dimensions. Since he is from the spirit world and only has a spirit body without an earthly form, he has had to learn about and experience earthly life through me. Many things are novel to him on Earth.

One day while Aesina and I were taking a walk outdoors, she said that Jullian was very excited, like a child, running and bouncing in front of us, and admiring the flowers along the trail. Aesina had the ability to see him. Wherever we went, he would rush ahead of us, eager to get to the next destination. He would gradually learn about manners and concepts in our society such as "ladies first."

One time, Aesina and I went to dine at an oceanfront restaurant, as Jullian liked to play in the ocean. I asked Jullian jokingly through Aesina, "Do you have chest hair like many human men?" According to Aesina, Jullian immediately grabbed a handful of finely curled seaweed and placed it on his chest. "Look! I also have chest hair!" He excitedly exclaimed.

Aesina and I burst into uncontrollable laughter at his witty and humorous innovation.

Whenever Aesina and I were together, Jullian was always a wonderful companion, patiently accompanying us in silence and with respect. Once, he could not hold back any longer and asked Aesina to convey to me that he would like to own a credit card like mine. Upon inquiry, he told us that he saw how convenient and magical my card was, as I could shop and dine to my heart's content. I had neglected to explain to him that it was a "credit" card, which meant I had to pay back all the expenditures from my bank account.

Jullian proudly presented us with his masterpiece a few weeks later. According to Aesina's description and the picture she drew, it was a credit card made of platinum, not plastic, soft topaz in color, surrounded with two rows of diamonds, and with pink polka dots in the center of the card. It was designed in the colors and style I liked. It was indeed a glittering and unique credit card. I used my thought to communicate with Jullian: *It is really creative. However, it cannot be used on Earth without activation.* I truly appreciate what I call the J (Jullian) *style* of humor.

One evening when Aesina and I were having dinner, we thought it might be nice to have our dessert at a nearby bakery. As we were enjoying the food and conversation, Aesina suddenly interrupted and said with embarrassment, "Jullian wants us to rush."

I was rather displeased and said of Jullian, "Doesn't he know it is very impolite to hasten us in the middle of our meal?" Jullian responded through Aesina, "In the spirit world, Nena (my spiritual name) is never so harsh to me."

While I was driving to the bakery, Aesina, with her eyes closed, described what she saw thus:

"I see a cake in the shape of a cup ornamented with a long stick on top."

We soon realized why Jullian had hurried us during our dinner. We arrived at the bakery just five minutes before they closed. A very creative chocolate cake in a cup shape adorned with a long straw-like chocolate bar attracted our attention immediately. It seemed that when we decided on the bakery, Jullian had rushed over there and selected what he liked. He had pressed us to hurry because the bakery was about to close for the day. I had misunderstood Jullian earlier and had self-righteously chastised him in front of Aesina.

In the spirit world, everyone gets along happily and lives in harmony, with mutual respect, care, and love. To Jullian, I am known as "Nena," his Heavenly mate, who would never be unkind to him. Due to the earthly role that I chose, as well as my limited understanding, I had ended up hurting his feelings. I felt ashamed and sent my sincere apology to Jullian with my thought.

I remember an occasion when I refused to communicate with Jullian for a whole day just because of some misunderstanding I had about him. Strangely, I kept feeling a tender warmth in the center of my chest. This wonderful loving energy stayed with me all day long. I knew Jullian was making every effort to appease me. I asked Aesina to let me know what Jullian was trying to tell me. His only words were, "I hope Nena does not feel bad anymore." Jullian did not say a single word in his own defense even though he had been misunderstood and wrongly reprimanded. He thought only of my feelings and cared for my welfare. I was truly moved by Jullian's sincerity, selflessness, and acceptance of me. I finally realized that true love is being thoughtful and wishing happiness for the other.

After that instance, I started looking at my earthly experience from the angle of the spirit world—from Jullian's Heavenly perspective. I learned to respect Jullian and give him time to observe and learn about life here on earth. In time, Jullian adapted to my earthly customs. He conducted himself appropriately, with respectful consideration for the situation. After several years together, Jullian behaved like a true gentleman: mature, composed, and well mannered. Moreover, he knew what was suitable to wear for different occasions. He showed his specific taste: elegant and stylish. He completely integrated into earthly living.

***

Being busy with my daily life, I often forget about Jullian's existence. However, a current of warm energy hugs my body before I open my eyes upon waking every morning. I know it is Jullian's way of saying good morning to me since it happens so regularly. Jullian uses this particular method to patiently guide me and help me learn that love needs no words or flowers to express itself—all it needs is a sincere heart.

My husband was very understanding on the day I told him about Jullian's existence. He was not shocked or threatened by this relationship but accepted it with ease. My husband could see that having Jullian in my life had turned me into a more loving person.

There are many interesting, heart-warming experiences I have had with Jullian over the years that I recall with fondness. They are all very precious to me. I am very grateful to Jullian for his total respect for me and for letting me be myself. Thanks to Jullian, I am able to earnestly carry out the role I have chosen for myself and work diligently on my earthly experiences.

9
The Thorny Rose

Broken Home

oth my parents were elementary school teachers in Taiwan. During my early childhood, they worked hard to support our family on meagre wages. After picking me up from kindergarten, they would buy dinner and drop me off at home. Then they would rush back to school for afterschool tutoring. They also tutored students at their homes in the evening. (At that time, it was a requirement to pass entrance exams from junior high school all the way to college.)

In kindergarten, I carried a key on a red string around my neck. I was a "latch key kid." When I got home from school, I would eat my dinner alone by a dim light, which was the typical type of lighting in homes at that time. The landlord had divided the apartment building into three rooms with wood partitions. We rented one room on the second floor nearest to the road where a night market was held. No one owned a TV at the time. Every night, I liked to lean against the window and watch the market in the soft streetlight below. Listening to the calling of the vendors, and hearing people chatting and laughing, I would fall gently to sleep.

I remember when I was in the first grade, waiting excitedly outside the delivery room in the hospital for my mother to give birth to my brother, Sam. I was happy to have a little brother. We are seven years apart. When Sam was five years old, we found out that his white blood cell count was overly high. Fifty years ago, this disorder was considered an incurable blood cancer. Whenever we visited him in the hospital, he would always ask, "Why do they keep changing the children next to my bed? Where did the other children go?"

We would tell white lies to comfort him and to cheer him up. I shared with Sam what I had learned from the Christian school I was attending at the time: "You can talk to God by saying prayers." I taught him a prayer and told him to say it frequently. Several weeks later, my brother's condition improved, and he eventually recovered completely. The love of God had created a beautiful miracle with Sam's pure heart and faith.

When I was in the fifth grade, my parents managed a children's clothing business in their spare time. This business failed the following year. Due to their irreconcilable differences, my parents got a divorce. Suddenly, my younger brother and I had to face a broken home and family bankruptcy. My brother stayed to live with my father, but I was taken away to live with my aunt and uncle. I also had to quit schooling.

I did not hear from my mother for about a year. I did not realize until adulthood that as the representative for the business, my mother was responsible for its financial matters. Having to repay the debt, she could not afford to care for my brother and me.

I was very grateful to my aunt and uncle for taking me in and caring for me for a while, along with their three children. My uncle's military retirement pension was very meager. To support their family, my aunt subsidized this income with a clothes alteration business.

Several months later, my father suddenly appeared at the door. He looked thin and haggard. I was anxious to go home with him again. But he took me to live at my grandfather's house so I could attend school. Grandfather had been living alone since grandmother passed away. It was an old brick house. The floor was concrete without tile. The toilet was in a hut separated from the main house. There was no television, no telephone, nor gas for cooking. We had to use firewood for cooking and boiled our drinking water. At night the house was lighted by a few dim light bulbs.

Whenever my grandfather went out for a walk at night, the timid me would hide inside my blanket and read my book with a flashlight. I often fell asleep while reading. Happily, I was able to go to school again! The elementary school was about a ten-minute walk away. Fortunately, I had only missed a few months of school and was able to catch up with my classmates.

In the second semester of sixth grade, my father came to my grandfather's house to take me home to live with him. My brother and I were finally reunited. My father took the place of our mother. He went grocery shopping, cooked, and washed our clothes after work.

I was always afraid of my father and dared not get near him. I will never forget the night my mother came to visit my brother and me. My drunken father tied my mother to a chair and whipped her with a belt. My brother and I hid in another room, crying with fear as we listened to our mother's painful screams. My heart ached, and I felt helpless. When the living room was quiet again, we knew my mother had left.

I was always filled with horror at nighttime when I heard my father's footsteps outside my bedroom door. He would come into my room and cover me with his huge body, drenched in the pungent smell of alcohol. He would forcefully kiss my mouth. I would then fight forcefully against him with all my might, kicking and hitting him. That seemed to wake him up a bit, so he would get up and leave my room. The same scenario repeated many times.

I missed my mother more and more each day. Finally, I gathered enough courage to let my father know that I wanted to take my brother with me to visit our mother for a few days. My brother and I stayed and lived with her from that day on. My father remarried a few years later and started another family. My brother and I would visit him and his new family when the school term was out.

To pay off the debt and support our family, my mother had to take on two jobs—as the manager of a restaurant and at a hotel night club. She usually left at noon and did not return home until one o'clock in the morning. We could only see her on weekends. My brother and I were happiest on my mother's rare days off. She would take us to popular Western restaurants and order combination dinners for the three of us to share.

***

It's easy to see how those traumatic experiences of my childhood would cause me pain and emotional imbalance. I often felt an emptiness in my heart. I longed for family warmth and yearned for love. And so, I got married one year after meeting my husband. There was fear in my heart, and this strongly affected my sense of self in my relationships. I would overly "package" myself to compensate for my insecurity and lack of confidence. Seeing others better off than me, I would get jealous. Viewing others' mistakes, I would criticize and blame them harshly and self-righteously, in order to maintain a false sense of superiority. Feeling superior is also a sign that one lacks self-confidence. I also attempted to conceal my guilt. I was afraid to face my own faults or let others find out about my mistakes. Moreover, I often verbally attacked and reprimanded others to safeguard my self-image. Everything I did was to protect that image.

Due to my insecurity, I was afraid of losing love, and thus, my desire to control others was born. I would use my own standards and expectations to make demands on others, hoping to compensate for the lack that I felt in my own heart. I received a temporary feeling of joy when others met my standards and expectations. However, I could not feel *Love*, because it was a conditional love and not the true love.

I was very willful and acted however I wanted to get my own way. My emotions were often triggered. My health was affected negatively by the long-term tension and stress. I knew inside that I must learn how to love myself and heal myself.

The Black Cat

I remember asking my mother while in elementary school, "Why am I given the nickname Black Cat?"

She explained, "You were born prematurely with darker skin. You had a bad temper since infancy. You would cry until your face turned red, even purple. Your father and I had to cautiously soothe your moods. We felt you were like a cute little black cat with its peculiar character."

I heard her clarification, yet I still wondered, why would my parents give me a bad temper instead of a good one? When I was young, I thought that having a bad temper was an inborn trait and unchangeable. Later, when I was married and had children of my own, I would vent my negative emotions without thinking when I felt angry. My husband would also raise his voice and speak to our boys in an accusatory tone. In response to such harsh words and negative emotions, our two sons would begin to cry and quarrel as well. The atmosphere in our family was filled with tension and unpleasantness much of the time. After we'd had a disagreement, my husband often said to me with a heavy heart, "You have never apologized even once since we got married." He was always the first to compromise to restore the peace.

At one point I had an extramarital affair. I was aware that what I did was against moral principles and conscience. However, to cover up my guilt, I blamed my unhappy past experiences for my marital discord. One day, I witnessed the man in this love affair betray me with another woman. I suffered tremendous anguish as my emotional turmoil and anger knotted itself like a ball in my chest. Upon arriving home, when I saw my husband sound asleep in bed, my tears streamed down uncontrollably. I hugged him and leaned on his shoulder. I wanted to tell him, *"I am sorry. I was wrong."* I knew I had hurt my husband's feelings, since he had seen my lover and me together. Now I was experiencing the emotion of my own betrayal. I was immersed in guilt and shame, for I had tried to deceive my husband. But now I took responsibility for my behavior. I told myself, *It is never too late.*

My husband has touched and changed me with his tender heart. I am truly grateful for his forgiveness. It is an absolute forgiveness, as he has never mentioned my affair or said a single word about the past.

Thereafter, I began to learn to be more truthful with myself and to be responsible for my behavior as well as for my negative feelings and emotions. Whenever negative emotional energy was seeking to burst out of my heart, I would ask myself, *Is there something I need to improve?* Being honest with myself has enabled my connection with my true self, which rapidly dissolved my negative emotions. I was finally able to say goodbye to my bad temper of over forty years.

Something wonderful happened recently. An old friend, whom I had not seen for several years, came to visit us. The first thing she said when entering our home was, "It feels different in your home. It feels so peaceful now." I never could have imagined it possible that the energy of our home would be transformed by the positive change in our hearts.

There is no perfect match between two people. The gap in a relationship is like a missing link in a circle. If not handled properly, the price to fix this gap can be very costly. I took a negative approach when I looked to the outside world to fill the gap, rather than looking within to heal myself. The only way to heal is to find the real cause, face my shortcomings with honesty, and start the change. By improving myself, I have made a huge difference in my marriage, which has had a positive ripple effect on my whole family. What I had once viewed as a marital crisis turned out to be a wake-up call and a blessing. It gave me the opportunity to learn how to become a better person. Happiness in marriage, like anything else, requires effort. I am truly grateful for this belated happiness!

10

The Transcendent Joy

A Precious Gift

*T*he telephone rang one March morning in 2014. It was my son Ricky, who told me that he had been throwing up for three days and could not ingest any food. The previous night a friend had taken him to see the doctor, who gave him some medication. His vision had become blurry from lack of food. Being too weak to drive himself to the store, he asked me to bring him some soft food and water with electrolytes.

I hung up the phone and quickly got dressed. Before stepping out of the house, I reminded myself not to forget the new blanket that I had just bought for Ricky. I knew he would need it to keep warm, especially when he was so frail.

Ricky came out to my car to greet me when I arrived his place. He insisted on helping me unload the groceries and carry them to his apartment. Being so weak from the illness, he dropped some of them on the way there. I hurried him inside and assured him that I could manage the rest on my own. I had not seen Ricky for several months. Now, he looked so much thinner than before. The luster was missing from his eyes, likely due to his illness. He seemed less healthy overall.

After carrying in the rest of the groceries, I went to his bedroom where he was resting and asked what he wanted to eat. "Applesauce," he said, looking grateful for my presence. I brought him a bowl of applesauce and felt comforted watching him slowly take one bite after another. I suddenly noticed there was only one pillow and a small blanket on the bed. Ricky explained that his girlfriend had moved out over one week ago. He started to cry and admitted that his bad temper had often made him quarrel with his girlfriend. They had got along very nicely at the beginning. However, the longer they were together, the less compatible they found each other.

Ricky said that he recalled hearing his father and me fighting when he was a child. He often fought with his younger brother, too. I had often scolded and punished him for his difficult behavior during his childhood. He told me that he had felt no warmth in the family. The unpleasant memories from his childhood haunted him like nightmares.

I began to cry as I listened to him, feeling immense regret for all that Ricky had suffered. I rebuked myself for not being able to see that my ill-temper and willfulness could hurt my children. Now I realize that a bad temper is an act of selfishness that is seeking to vent one's own emotions without respecting the other person's feelings.

Ricky wiped his eyes with his sleeve as he continued to talk: "I often blame myself for not having a good education. I would really like to attend college now, but I am worried about not being able to handle the school curriculum because I left school so long ago."

I said to him encouragingly, "Just do what your heart desires, and you will feel fulfilled and happy. Many things require personal participation before finding out if they are suitable for you or not."

I could see that Ricky was discrediting himself as he reminisced about his past actions, which he felt were dishonorable. Because of a drug issue, he had been put into a juvenile correction facility for a while. He lacked confidence in himself and often felt nervous and panicky without knowing the cause. He apologized to me for incurring lots of expenses for his sake.

I listened quietly. I could sense the pressure he was under, as well as the anger, conflict, and struggle that had tormented him all these years. When he finished talking, I asked him, "May I share a story with you, Ricky?" He nodded.

"When I was in junior high school, I had a very good friend named Hua. She and I both came from a single-parent home with our mothers busy working to support the families. There was no one home when we came back from school. So, we would hang out after school and return home when it was dark. Once Hua and I went into a small supermarket and saw imported ham inside the refrigerator. It was such a luxurious item for us, being from less affluent families. I took a ham and swiftly hid it inside my schoolbag when no one was paying attention. We left the store in a hurry and went directly to Hua's home to share the ham together. That was the first time we had done such a thing.

One week later, we deliberately looked for a different supermarket. We finally came across a small market. As soon as we walked in, we noticed the store was selling all sorts of imported food items, beyond anything we had ever imagined! We quickly grabbed two packages of ham but got busted by the storekeeper while we were trying to put them into our schoolbags. She notified the store owner.

Hua and I knew that we were in trouble. We kept our heads down nervously, worrying about the consequences. The owner walked toward us, and I heard her call out my name. I lifted my head with surprise. My face turned crimson red. The store owner was none other than my most beloved great aunt. I was filled with horrible shame, guilt, and regret. With my head bent low, I said to her, "I am very sorry."

I had concealed this story from everyone for over forty years. Not even my parents knew about it. I told Ricky that I now could appreciate this experience, because my shame became the force that awakened my conscience. It guided me toward the right path and helped me not make the same mistake again.

Ricky listened attentively as I continued.

"I made mistakes during my youth. These experiences are like scars that I am very scared to touch. It is because I always feel very remorseful and full of self-blame every time I recall them. I have experienced many imperfect 'MEs'."

I went on to explain that when I learned to face myself with honesty and forgive myself, the dirty stains from life became precious experiences that enabled me to accept and understand those with the same experiences.

I looked at Ricky and said, "I no longer live in the shadow of my past. What others see is the present me. My current thoughts and actions determine the future me, as long as I am willing to cherish the present moment. There are plentiful 'presents' that offer numerous opportunities so that I can become a better me."

I apologized to Ricky sincerely: "I am sorry to have given you an unhappy childhood. I beg your forgiveness." I then asked him, "Do you think my temper has improved during these past years?"

"Yes," he answered, "I don't see you get upset anymore."

I explained to him that everyone needs to learn to be responsible for themselves. That the setbacks we encounter in life are opportunities for us to reexamine ourselves.

"Your father and I never blamed you," I said, "because we felt the pain you were going through, as well as the struggles inside your heart and your body. We understand that it requires a lot of courage and perseverance to start over, to take one step at a time, and get back up when we fall. We see many merits in you. We believe in you and your efforts deserve our respect. We trust you can overcome your challenges. We will always support you and cheer you. Our love will always be with you."

Ricky wiped his tears and smiled.

***

Two weeks later, my husband was the main chef in charge of our dinner one night. As he cooked his gourmet dish, I acted as his assistant, preparing the side dishes, and cleaning up. Suddenly, the phone rang. It was Ricky. He invited us to join him and his friends for dinner. I explained that we were already cooking dinner but thanked him for the invitation and asked him to give our regards to his friends.

My heart was filled with joy when I hung up the phone. That was the first time in a long while that Ricky had shown a willingness to initiate goodwill toward us. I was so delighted to know that the knot in his heart had been released. Even though it was just a phone call, it had great meaning. His act of acceptance had melted away decades of deadlock between us and brought us closer. I am so thankful for this precious gift.

Blessings in Disguise

In the summer of 2014, my husband and I went on a month-long vacation in Asia. Upon returning home, we found Ricky at home with a kitten he had brought with him. He had decided to move back home for a while, as the lease on his apartment was about to expire. He explained that he had used up all of his

The Loving Connection

savings after moving out two years ago. He hoped to save some money by moving back home.

Our home suddenly became very lively. My younger son and his girlfriend had been living with us since the summer of 2013, and now Ricky and his kitten would be living with us too. With my husband semi-retired, we had thought that we would have our world to ourselves, keeping each other company and traveling together. However, life did not turn out according to our expectations. With five people living together, besides the overstuffed refrigerator, there were frequently dirty dishes in the kitchen sink and used glasses all over the house. Many items were not placed back in their proper locations; dirty socks were scattered about, and clothing was left in the washing machine or dryer.

My husband and I decided to set up rules of responsibility, hoping that everyone would cooperate and keep our home in order. I could not understand why anyone would fail to meet the basic accountability. I also wondered whether to keep the cat or find a new home for it, as I had never cared for a cat before. With our love for Ricky, my husband and I decided to keep the cat and began to learn about its characteristics and preferences.

My emotions went up and down while taking care of the family chores. I pondered how to communicate with my family. Then I remembered some words of wisdom from a couple who had been married for over fifty years: *Home is a place about loving, not a place for reasoning.* Home is a safe haven for us to rest, to recharge, and to release stress. The warmth of home gives us motivation and helps us start afresh every day with a positive attitude.

When I woke up in the morning, I began to say an affirmation: *This is a wonderful day. I choose to do everything with a happy heart.* No longer would I use my ego to judge good or bad, right or wrong, but would face everything with calmness and acceptance. I would ask myself, *What can I do for others?* rather than asking what the other person could do for me. I felt very fulfilled when I gave love without assessing how the others should feel or expecting them to reciprocate.

Moreover, I began exploring how to find inner peace through my daily association with my family. Wonderful things started happening. I would receive messages intuitively, as if being guided by an inner wisdom. The first thing I practiced was respect. The practice of feeling respect for everything and everyone helped me to attain spiritual freedom and restore my heart's equilibrium. I also learned to respect myself. I made sure to leave room to love and be kind to myself, while providing love to my family.

Without my attachment to negative emotions, I discovered that everyone has a different definition for their standard of neatness, based on a person's lifestyle and habits. Everyone is also at a different level of maturity and awareness; hence, the different perceptions and behaviors. I respect that every individual has personal choices, favorites, and their own growing pace. Previously, I had applied my egoic standards and viewed everything from within my own limited framework. I was arrogant and gleeful when others met my standards and expectations. But when they failed, I became angry and disappointed, even furious. As a result, I was letting others control my emotions and happiness.

Ironically, after we lose a loved one, we hold on to our fond memories of them, not the unpleasant ones. That is because we can recognize their value and importance, as we are no longer judging this person with our ego. The ego's judgment had limited our love.

Once I removed my egoic standards, my heart began to soften, and I became more flexible. I learned to use humor and understanding to communicate with my family. Now I evaluated my progress in terms of my growing awareness. When I regressed to my old thinking mode and habitual behavior, I would encourage myself with these words: *This is a normal learning process as long as I am on the right track.*

One day I said to my husband, "I've finally figured out what it means to keep one eye closed when looking at things." He listened to me with curiosity. I continued, "I used to hold a magnifying glass up to the other person and clearly see the shortcomings and areas needing further improvement in them. It would place pressure not only on others but also on myself. I started to practice closing one eye every day when viewing things. Interestingly, with one eye closed, I can see more clearly the other person's improvements, even if it is only one percent." My husband looked at me with an understanding smile.

Indeed, family members feel respected and encouraged when there is no blame or pressure put on them to change.

Ricky began to open up. Sometimes, he would come to the kitchen and chat about his condition. One time he said to me, "I wake up every morning with my thoughts running back to many unpleasant experiences in the past. My mood becomes one of frustration, worrying about the many tasks to complete. I start to sweat nervously fearing I cannot make it. I must spend thirty minutes on overcoming my fear and nervousness before I can get out of the bed."

There were big ups and downs for Ricky, often depending on the medication he was taking for depression. We felt comforted when Ricky explained that he had found a prescription that worked: "I have to take two weeks to gradually reduce the dosage of my old medication before stopping that medicine. Then I need to adjust new medication every two weeks. I am very happy there is finally a medication that suits me without side effects. I am starting to gain physical strength, and feel motivated to interact with my friends, and I want to begin exercising."

Ricky enjoyed sharing his life experiences more and more. My husband and I sensed his huge change. He now showed trust in my husband and me. Facing himself honestly, he admitted to using rebellious behavior as a protest and to demonstrate his dissatisfaction. He also expressed regret for getting expelled from high school due to drug possession. He had now matured to a point where he realized that he was being controlled by negative emotions, not by his true self.

My husband and I had learned to be good listeners, as our son was not always willing to communicate with us. It was also difficult for him to express his feelings or opinions. Therefore, I would stop myself immediately at times when I was anxious to express my opinion, fearing I would forget what I wanted to say. I would be careful not to interrupt Ricky or stray from the topic of his conversation. With patient listening, we could better understand the point he desired to make and what was troubling him. We would thus offer the appropriate parental guidance. We believed that with careful irrigation, the seed of love in his heart would sprout, grow, and strive to be a tree.

There was a weekend when Ricky shut himself in his room for two days. He did not leave his room and didn't interact with the family. He was resentful and impatient when we inquired about his well-being. The morning of the third day, he finally showed up in the kitchen.

I asked him gently, "Do you have anything to talk about? Your father and I could sense your troubled heart."

Ricky became emotional as tears filled his eyes: "I felt I had already worked very hard, but why did everything go back to its original point again?"

He recounted a recent series of obstacles that had caused tremendous stress and confusion inside him. I listened attentively, contemplating how to help him and give him hope and strength. Suddenly, something touched my heart. It was the resonance of love—not sympathy, not pity, but an understanding.

I told Ricky, "I understand your struggles, your efforts, the hardship you have suffered, and the journey of your heart."

The light of hope shot out of Ricky's eyes. Raising his voice, he asked excitedly: "Do you understand? Do you truly understand?"

I answered with conviction, "My heart felt it completely!"

He came over and hugged me. Then he said, "I am hungry. Would you cook a poached egg for me? I have been indoors for days and would like to go out for some exercise."

Looking at Ricky eagerly preparing to go out, I knew his dark inner cloud had dissipated.

***

To overcome the troubles brought on by his disorder, Ricky had started learning capoeira, the Brazilian martial art, and it ignited his passion for life. After learning the handstand, he practiced at different locations and had photos taken of himself. We knew he had found his confidence. He also began to develop his spiritual beliefs and participated in charitable activities to share his love.

Whenever I saw my husband talking to Ricky with a gentle tone and guiding him with patient kindness, I would give my husband the thumbs-up. I exclaimed, "So beautiful! How did you do that?" I had witnessed his transformation from a quick-tempered young man to a kind and loving father. I finally realized that there is a kind of love that uses challenges to help the other person grow and find inner love. When we learn to practice not only respect and acceptance, but also understanding, we discover the value hidden in our experiences.

Eternal Love from Ricky

In the middle of October 2016, my father passed away, and my husband and I flew to Taiwan. My husband went out of town for a few days while I stayed in Taiwan to take care of matters related to my recently deceased father. One morning, I received a phone call from my younger son from the United States. His voice was choking with tears as he tried to speak:

"Mom, are you home? Mom, would you please sit down. Please be strong . . . Ricky had not gone to work for one week. We could not contact him through his phone. We asked the police to go to his apartment. They found Ricky on the living room floor. Mom, Ricky has passed away . . ."

I tried to end the call with calmness. There was no warning sign. I was totally unprepared for this. We had just celebrated his thirty-third birthday before leaving the United States. How could Ricky be gone forever? How could this have happened in just a few weeks? I asked myself, *Is this true?* I sat alone in shock. A fierce pain surged from the depths of my heart. Tears flooded from my eyes. I was overwhelmed by sorrow, wondering why this had happened and feeling the terrible hopelessness.

My husband called that evening to ask about Ricky. With concern in his voice, he said to me, "I heard that Ricky did not go to work for a week. Were you able to get hold of him?"

I decided to use a white lie because I didn't want to worry him just then, "I think he must be on vacation. I remember him mentioning some arrangement for his vacation. There is no problem. Please don't worry." I planned to tell my husband about Ricky when he returned so I could be with him and hold his hands.

I believed that a mother and son could connect through their hearts during the period he was crossing over. I did not feel anxious or uneasy. I called Aesina and told her what had happened. The first question that came out of my mouth was, "Did Ricky go back to Heaven?"

"Yes," she said.

She conveyed this message when I asked her to connect Ricky with me:

"Ricky is very happy as he is in a state of Heavenly vibration. Peace and love dwell deep in his heart. He wants you to know that he loves you very much. He appreciates all that you had given him, which was abundant and meaningful. His subconscious knew you were ready and would be able to handle his choice in ending his earthly life. He had fulfilled his purpose on Earth and does not wish any of his loved ones to feel sad for him. The greatest comfort for him is that you know and affirm that he is a very courageous soul.

"He used his own methods to help you. He had accomplished whatever plan he had intended and was ready to let go now. He had gone through very tough challenges on Earth. However, his spirit is not under shock or trauma. He does not need healing from Archangel Benny. Everything is perfect!

"He cares about his earthly parents and is concerned about your grief. You and your husband must calm down. You shouldn't worry anymore, and you should let go. He would be worried too if you are sad, and he would not be able to let go either. He will be relieved if you are happy. He can communicate with you when you are still.

"Please understand and respect his choice of terminating his earthly life. He wishes you to be happy for him and wants you to celebrate his life with a joyful heart filled with love and understanding. Please do not keep his material possessions as there are lots of memories and other attachments with them. They do not serve his eternal purpose anymore."

Ricky also expressed his gratitude to Aesina for passing these messages to me.

Aesina continued to deliver the messages from Heaven:

"The Earth is a school that enables humans to learn. If humans stay in ignorance, fear, or guilt for a long period of time, they will begin to deny their essence of love. Their body, mind, and soul can become imbalanced, as they cannot resonate with the love of the heart for a long time. When they leave their physical form on Earth, their spirit will be in a space devoid of love. They are like lost children who cannot find their way home. However, if they open their heart to their true self and pray, light, love, and truth will guide them home."

***

At Ricky's farewell ceremony, we conducted it as a celebration. We celebrated a courageous spirit that had come to Earth to experience what he wanted to learn. He had fulfilled his higher purpose. He thus felt that he could opt out. He had returned to Heaven, our spirit home, full of love, joy, and beauty.

We fully respected Ricky's choice because we believed it was the best option for him. He was a messenger of love who came to our family to help us learn forgiveness, understanding, and love. He enabled us to find our inner love. Love will continue to be passed on to one another.

After the ceremony, Aesina came to me and told me, "Ricky was present at this memorial service. He was standing in the middle front of the room, dressed in a suit, and looked very happy."

Even though we and Ricky are in different dimensions, the love is never lost between us. Love is forever in our hearts.

The best gift we can give Ricky now is to get past our grief and sadness, and accept the fact that he is no longer with us on Earth with peace and harmony in our hearts.

We can communicate with Ricky directly through our thoughts, as thought is a very powerful energy. My husband and I sometimes invite Ricky to join us in the activities that we know were his favorites while on Earth. I know Ricky is with us whenever I feel warm energy on the left side of my body and in the middle of my chest. The love between Heaven and Earth has never been severed.

Every process in life, each experience and memory, every kind of emotion and feeling—all are very precious. Our laughter, pain, anger, sadness, helplessness, and fear can make deep impressions on our hearts, like rich colors on a lively painting. When we can totally accept and surrender to the full expression of our life, our hearts will emanate the beautiful light of love, wisdom, courage, and strength to resonate deeply with others.

II

Beauty All Around

Miss Ego

I received a gift from the Heavenly Parents in the spiritual administration Aesina and I held in September 2011. They gave me a pink crystal heart and counseled me to cherish it. I felt a very warm energy in the middle of my chest but did not understand its significance.

Thereafter, I often pondered the meaning of this pink crystal heart, and I wanted to know why it created different emotional sensations in the middle of my chest. I noticed that my heart would contract and shift from a state of peace and tranquility to a feeling of pressure whenever I attempted to endorse the importance of my "I" by receiving praise and validation for my contribution. It also happened whenever "I" used my perception to judge someone as right or wrong, or applied comparison to determine good or bad. Also, whenever "I" expected a receive-for-a-give, and imposed guilt or obligation on another person: *You should . . .* My heart also felt pressure whenever "I" was eager to show off, whenever "I" sensed my self-esteem being threatened, and whenever "I" felt guilty.

I realized it was the energy current of our ego that produces negative emotions in our hearts. Whenever our heart is under pressure, it seeks an outlet for this negative energy. Our words and behavior will thus tend to be competitive, flashy, accusing, and aggressive. When ego is taking the lead, it will influence our thoughts and cognition and hinder our correct judgment and analytical ability.

Once I understood how the ego works, I started to closely observe my thoughts to see whether they were positive or negative. As our thoughts and emotions affect each other, correcting the negative thoughts can transform our emotions and feelings. I also check to see whether my heart feels peaceful and calm, or feels a current of pressure, whenever I express "I". If that happens, I consciously slow down my speech and choose my words more carefully.

After observing my pink crystal heart for a long time, I finally understood the sacred nature of my heart. It has become my habit to observe the feelings of my heart, which helps me to recognize my emotions and distinguish the little me (my ego) from my true self. I am grateful to the Heavenly Parents for guiding and inspiring me.

I started making friends with my ego by facing it with honesty, without resistance or guilt. I humorously called it "Miss Ego" with mock politeness. Whenever my heart shifts from calmness to tense energy, I know Miss Ego is using the negative emotions to remind me that I have departed from love and my divine essence.

Ego is the source of our fear, lack, unhappiness, hurt, and neglected self. It uses negative emotions to express itself, which are the unadulterated reactions inside us. Ego craves our attention and acceptance. We can embrace it gently and say, "I am sorry for letting you live in fear for a long time. I am willing to take responsibility for everything I do. Thank you for reminding me of the areas where I need to improve, release, and balance."

Ego is a part of us. What we should do is to love it completely. We will then begin to discover that ego acts as the messenger of love. These negative emotions from ego provide lessons for us to reexamine ourselves and to learn from. Our awareness of the ego's messages helps our heart return to peace and harmony.

Activation of the Spirit Body

During the spiritual administration with Aesina in December 2012, I experienced the creation of my spirit. The Heavenly Parents created my spirit body to dwell within my physical body. Throughout the entire process, my body felt very light and pure, as if wrapped inside a warm energy. I strongly sensed the love from the Heavenly Parents. They told me that this spirit body was not yet ready, as it had just been formed and was still fragile. I was told to be mindful and create beautiful thoughts to protect this spirit body. I also needed to keep its energy positive by filling it with love, peace, and joy.

One week later, Aesina met me with tear-filled eyes, and said, "I learned from the Heavenly Parents that I must *activate* your spirit body this morning. I am very touched and grateful as it is such an honor. I hope I don't disappoint them."

After saying the prayer to the Heavenly Parents, Aesina told me a golden light was entering my crown chakra to fill into this spirit body.

Next, she said, "Every speck of light is energy that gives the life force to the spirit. I see the color of your essence; a soft pink light emanating all over your spirit body now that it is activated. The blue light, the light of healing that everyone has, is now emitting from your spirit body. Here comes the topaz color, which is the color of your Heavenly mate Jullian, to enable you to resonate with each other. Your light will grow brighter as you continue to evolve spiritually."

The Gift of Talents

In August 2013, I was very grateful to receive the energy of my talents in our Spiritual Administration. The Heavenly Parents infused a variety of colored lights through my crown chakra into every cell of my spirit body, as well as into the center of my sacred heart, shaped like a goose egg. Aesina conveyed the following message from them:

"Your talents are created according to your free will. Thus, you know your own talents. Each talent holds a different energetic wave and color. We will strengthen your talents according to your needs.

Your talents are visible in the spirit world. However, they can be obvious or restricted on Earth according to your blueprint. Sometimes, personal efforts will be needed in order to release them. This setup is full of significance, as lots of your talents and all earthly experiences resonate and cooperate with each other."

The Heavenly Parents continued earnestly:

"Use these talents wisely. Do you know the reason why we infused the energy of talents into your spirit cells and your heart? When you share your talents and serve others with love, your talents will shine, grow, and get strengthened. That is why these talents exist. They are beautiful gifts that require careful application so that they do not become a burden."

Our talents can enrich life and beautify the world. When we serve with love, our talents empower the loving connection between people, and enable us to share our joy with others.

I am so thankful for this precious and loving gift.

Connecting with Our Inner Self

In September 2015, Aesina told me that our spiritual administration that day would be held outdoors. She already knew the place where it would take place.

I recalled the first time we had held our spiritual administration in a public setting back in 2013. It had taken place indoors in a quiet room at a hotel. The Heavenly Mother had chosen a "question and answer" format, rather than have Aesina channel the messages. I still remember the first question: *"What is Heaven to you?"* I had answered every question based on my level of my awareness at the time.

I was curious and excited about our first outdoor spiritual administration. We went to a busy and noisy tourist location downtown near the ocean. We sat on a bench outside a store selling Western style items. I closed my eyes to calm my thoughts. My heart began to feel warm. I knew the spirit world was ready for us. I then heard Aesina pray to the Heavenly Parents, offering gratitude as usual:

"Thank you for guiding us to this type of environment in order to teach us how to disengage ourselves from the hustle and bustle around us. Therefore, we can focus on what we need to hear, accept, and feel. We appreciate this new experience and training so that we can learn how to connect with our inner self . . ."

She began the administration and said the following:

"The gentle, bright white light entering through your crown chakra is to cleanse you. Go into your inner self to feel the pure beauty of the spirit by freeing yourself from the distraction of this particular environment. You shall find the State of Heaven when you continue to explore and connect deeply within your spirit.

Take a deep breath and relax in order to sense the existence of the spirit in your body. The spirit has a little weight. It is an element with its own quality that is unlike any human body or anything on Earth.

Spirit confined itself in our body to help us move and function through the operation of its mind. Our feeling actually is the feeling of the spirit. True happiness is found by going deep into the 'heart' of the spirit.

This 'heart' is the library of wisdom that manages our thoughts and physical reactions, as well as assists us in our behaviors and all feelings. Everyone inside the world of the spirit shall witness the beauty and wholeness of all things. What a great and powerful master this heart is! So wise and so perfect our spirit and our heart are!

Now, sense the beauty, wisdom, and power of the spirit when you take a deep breath. Express the wisdom and power of the spirit through your physical experiences. This is the union of the body and spirit."

After the ceremony, I said to Aesina, "This location is very suitable. I heard the sound of pedestrians passing and talking at the beginning of the ceremony. However, I felt everything become very quiet soon afterward. Was it because no tourists were passing here during our administration?"

Aesina smiled and said, "Many tourists were passing by continuously, and there were also people talking and children laughing throughout our process. You will know the situation when you go home and listen to our recording."

So, my dedication to the spiritual administration had insulated me from the outer world at that time. I learned from this experience that we can connect with our inner self, which is undisturbed by the outer world, when we totally relax, empty our thoughts, and go deep into that ultimate peace and tranquility in our heart. There are many ways to connect with our inner self—through prayer, meditation, breathing, being in nature, or simply by living in the present.

Heaven on Earth

It was a sunny fall morning in November of 2015. Aesina drove me to a resort lined with tall palm trees in a tropical landscape. We saw ducks swimming happily in the ponds and resting on the banks beside a pagoda. Birds were singing cheerfully and flying playfully from tree to tree. Nature presented a lovely picture of peace, tranquility, and harmony.

After saying the prayer of invocation, Aesina conveyed the message from the spiritual realm:

"The Heavenly Parents inspired us to come to this place because you are writing about body, mind, and spirit. They want us to know that all these surroundings, the trees, bushes, flowers, water, rocks, soil, birds, and insects, are also spirits created by them as humans were. They all can feel love and sense our emotions, whether positive or negative.

Their energetic vibration is different from human beings as they have different functions. Like everything that exists in nature, their function is to assist in completing our mission: the important and great mission of the Universe. These spirits also serve us and help us fulfill our higher purpose. They are part of us, and we are part of them.

Do not ignore, waste, or abuse them, but love them. They have their own body, mind, and feelings, as they are spirits like us. We should use our feelings and thoughts to communicate with them because they are living beings with loving vibrations. They will continue serving us when we cherish and take care of them with gratitude.

Indians knew this a long time ago. They worship the Earth and Mother God because they know we are 'One Spirit.'

Everyone has the responsibility to take care of the spirits created by the Heavenly Parents. We must respect them as they are our equals. They are also our spirit brothers and sisters with different forms to help us in our lives. They not only give us food and nutrients for our body, but also give our spirit joy, happiness, and healing.

Now open your heart and mind and communicate with them from the deepest part of your soul and with a peaceful heart. Listen to them carefully. Listen to their whispers. Their love is so pure and beautiful. You can give them love in return. This is the power of mutual support. This purpose and guidance is important for the loving connection."

These messages inspired me. Whenever I visit my garden in the morning, I begin by praising, blessing, and thanking the birds' songs, flowers, trees, fruit, clouds in the sky, the sun, air, and breeze. I usually focus on the present moment in my life. I praise the decor in my home, and I tell my dishes how beautiful they are while washing them. When cooking, I give thanks to my food. I even thank my garbage as I dump it in the bin for completing its service to us.

Each connection made with love and gratitude empowers the flow of energy between us and others. Our heart is thus filled with peace, joy, harmony, contentment, and abundance. Life is designed to serve all. The grace of love is everywhere.

Message of Love from Our Heavenly Parents

The following section is a "summary" drawn from the messages that we have received from the Heavenly Parents and recorded at our spiritual administration sessions since 2012. We hope that you will reflect on this spiritual wisdom and guidance to support you in your own growth and development as a Heavenly Spirit.

Every spirit is created with the Heavenly Parents' divine DNA and according to everyone's free will. There are billions of spirit cells in your spirit body. Every spirit cell is the Heavenly Parents' love. Every spirit is an expression of wholesome and perfect love.

Besides free will, every spirit is given its own "spiritual blueprint," which determines its characteristics and needs at the moment of its creation. The Heavenly Parents also know the specific desires of each spirit: the various ways it wants to develop and the different ideas it wishes to express after its creation. The spirit is created and born after accepting its own specific spiritual blueprint.

This baby spirit grows like a human child and stops when it reaches the perfect state. During its period of growth, the spirit begins to explore itself and develop. Guardian angels, personal care angels, and all kinds of nurturing angels will continue to assist in the spirit's growth. The spirit will learn from different mentors as well, according to its wishes. The growth and development process of the earthly baby is based on the model of how its spirit grows and develops.

The growth and development of the spirit not only applies to the individual but also affects the whole. Spirits are connected with each other and with the *All* through light and love, as love has no barrier and neither has light. Every spirit is full of infinite love and light as it was created by the Heavenly Parents, who are sourced from the Universe. Therefore, the spirit has its own uniqueness but is also connected with everything as a whole.

Every spirit has its own unique vibrational formulation and energy field. It possesses its own thoughts, ideas, and resonance. Different spirits form a beautiful contrast with each other and highlight each other's importance and value. That is why every spirit is so precious.

Just like your physical body, your spirit requires you to nurture it and keep it clean. Therefore, you need to keep your thoughts positive and use this powerful energy from the mind. You also must keep the spirit heart peaceful, tranquil, joyful, and grateful. They are like vitamins for the spirits that give them the power to function properly.

You can talk to your heart often: "I love you and thank you because you are a gift of love from the Heavenly Parents. You are a messenger from Heaven. You are the treasure of Heaven. Your beauty lights up the world."

Live every day happily. Coming to Earth gives you cause to celebrate every experience with joy. Celebrate even the tears, as sadness provides depth, much in the same way that happiness does. Every feeling and emotion is precious and worth celebrating. To feel is the function of the spirit. Feelings can reach the most beautiful and peaceful depth. Because of feelings, the spirit can sense your emotions in life. This is the source of inspiration for creating art, music, and literature.

Emotions and feelings are both important, so you must apply wisdom to maintain an equilibrium between them. You also need to use love to blend both together into a beautiful harmony. You must keep your body, mind, and spirit in balance and should not use your minds only to analyze, as it tends to be narrow and limiting.

You also need to keep your heart open to comprehend and experience with the body. Your most beautiful true self will express itself naturally when your body, heart, and spirit are in unity. That means you have already invited Heaven into your heart and into your life experiences. Therefore, take time to appreciate the sensation of perfection and begin to notice the wisdom, light, beauty, significance, and the messages that are present in everything.

Every day when you wake up, take a deep breath and inhale beauty, happiness, and wisdom. Feel gratitude for your life. Exhale any sorrow, worry, doubt, or stress that plagues you. Open your heart to welcome in all the beautiful energy. Embrace, support, and blend into this energy. This will help to enhance your light, expand your love, and increase your confidence. Consequently, you will no longer be affected by the outer world.

Relax your whole body at bedtime. Exhale all the experiences from the day, release them like flowing water. Tell yourself that you have done your best. Tomorrow you will wake up refreshed. The cells of your body are constantly renewing. You will have a new world with new experiences.

Behold every second, every minute, and every day. Greet every day with ease, live the desired experience, then let it go. You will feel more and more free. And with this freedom, you will enjoy the bliss, peace, purity, and perfection of your spirit. Your physical body will also feel healthy and happy.

Life experience is very challenging from the human perspective. Yet, it is splendid from the spiritual standpoint. Your body, heart, and spirit, as well as your thoughts and emotions, coordinate with your original soul agreement that you planned for the highest good of everything. Despite the physical challenges on Earth, when you accomplish much of what you have planned in the spirit world, your soul will celebrate all of your hard work and achievements. When you are in alignment with your divine purpose, your vibrational frequency rises, and your soul is fulfilled.

You desire to return to your true self in every earthly life. If you work to attain that, you can reach your soul's most beautiful state. Every experience in your earthly life is there to help you return home to the moment when your spirit was created. Your spirit will shout with exultation: "Yes! I AM!" When this happens, you can feel truly free, peaceful, and joyful. You will feel whole and complete. The highest realm is profoundly pure, peaceful, and abundant. This is the real Heaven where pure beauty and true love reside.

Embrace all and give it your all. Do so without hesitation and doubt. Do not filter and diminish or cloud your experience through the thinking mind. When your heart is pure and at peace, everything is beautiful to you. All that comes in and goes out is perfect just as it is.

The Heart is love. Love is Heaven. You can bring Heaven to every human mind, human life, and human heart. There is no division between Heaven and Earth, neither is there any separation between Heaven and human beings. All blend together and create perfect harmony.

Be grateful that you are a beautiful spirit with beautiful energy. Be thankful for opportunities to help others, and share your love, beauty, and joy with them. Gratitude is the way love communicates. You should not feel grateful only when you receive benefits or when the energy of your experience feels positive. It is not only positive energy that serves to nurture us. There is great value in the opposite, as you can learn and grow from negative energy. That is because the dichotomy of darkness and light is necessary to sustain the energy of our light.

When your heart is filled with unconditional gratitude, feeling it in your every inhalation and exhalation, joy fills every one of your cells. Gratitude promotes respect, understanding, and acceptance. Gratitude softens everything, makes everything come alive, and brings beauty to the relationships between people and every being on Earth. Gratitude is a beautiful energy that strengthens your love for deep meaningful connections.

You are closely interrelated with each other. Your every move, thought, expression of happiness, or spiritual inspiration connects with that of all others. This is the "loving connection" that has always existed.

You are in alignment with your spirit and have reached a state of Oneness whenever you imbue unconditional love into everything in your life; your thoughts, words, actions, behaviors, and beingness. Oneness—with perfection of spirit through unconditional love and accepting without judgment— is the ultimate state that your spirit and energy desire to achieve.

Your earthly experience will resonate with your spirit, heart, and the whole spiritual realm. By sharing all the wisdom, knowledge, and experiences with one another, the Universe thus expands and is enriched.

True Self ~ Love, Peace, Joy, Beauty

The message received by Aesina in the spiritual administration held in April 2015 was powerful: *"Our Heavenly Parents endowed us with the essence of Love, Peace, Joy, and Beauty upon our creation, which is our true self. How we utilize these four elements to find our true self and true happiness through our life experiences is the greatest purpose and the meaning of life."*

The messages from this administration inspired me to explore the meaning of our true self. I understand from my deep reflection on this wisdom that we can only find our true self from within. Our true self is very precious and perfect.

Our Heavenly Parents created our spirit and our heart of eternal joy. The heart is our true self. We are always searching for love and happiness externally, and we forget that we already possess them within us. Happiness is our essence and already exists. It does not rely on any external things in our environment. Unhappiness is sourced from not loving ourselves truly.

Generally speaking, we pursue happiness through material things when we are not yet awakened. However, doing so only provides short-lived satisfaction; longing and desires will soon reappear. This condition is caused by the feeling of lack due to the imbalance of the heart. Happiness would be an illusion for those who use material things to fill the emptiness of their heart. When we become grateful for everything we have, we will realize that gratitude is the connector to love. The energy of gratitude will reward us by enriching our heart and granting us true happiness.

We are multi-dimensional and eternal beings. We exist in countless life forms and consciousness at the same time. Therefore, there are differences such as little self, true self, and higher self. Our spirit uses a portion of its energy, gets veiled, and forgets its sacred essence when coming to the Earth in order to experience itself through duality. Consequently, our heart begins to have two "*mes*." One of them is the true self with the unity consciousness of the spiritual dimension. The other is the ego (little self) with the separation consciousness that exists on the third and fourth dimension.

Love presents itself in a two-faceted way: true self and ego. We cannot deny either one. Ego serves us and enables us to experience ourselves at a different level of consciousness. It also uses negative emotions to remind us and help us awaken spiritually to our true self. The emotions and feelings are our best guidance from the heart. Every kind of emotion is valuable. Therefore, we should not only respect and accept every aspect of our emotions, but also feel and listen with honesty to the messages they intend to convey.

The negative emotions felt in the heart are a sign that our mode of thinking and belief are held in binary opposition. We use "good/bad, right/wrong, success/failure" to judge ourselves, people, events, things, and everything around us. We also often apply the idea of "reciprocal relationship" to view the interactions between people. We are thus limiting love and happiness by staying within a self-customized framework. This is not real but an illusion, and not true love. It's the separation consciousness that ego produces. However, true love encompasses both perfection and imperfection. True love has no place for comparison, judgment, blame, or punishment. True love is unconditional.

When we are unable to face or accept certain aspects of ourselves, they become negative emotions hidden in our heart. Every negative emotion provides us the opportunity to re-examine problems. Our heart will soften and have space if we are willing to be true to ourselves, and then ask ourselves, *Is there something I need to improve?* Sometimes inspiration or intuition will appear when we need to break through certain blind spots. Sometimes certain words or paragraphs in an article we read will particularly attract our attention, as they are guiding us to the answers we need. Our heart is the treasure chest of our wisdom. When our heart is in peace and harmony, it will connect with the spiritual wisdom and enable us to see the truth.

Our heart possesses light and divine love, as well as darkness (fear), in accord with the binary opposition on the Earth. Darkness is a part of us—it is our shadow self. Darkness can appear through painful experiences in a past life or childhood, including but not limited to the frustrations and defeats that we encounter in life. These are the hidden emotions that we have suppressed for a long time, including our guilt. This shadow self is the imbalanced and disharmonious energy that we need to face and get to know. Only through love and forgiveness can we release it.

Profound meaning is hidden within every surfacing of the darkness. Darkness as the opposite of light exists to serve the light. It has a very important role in our soulful evolution, as it offers the experiences needed for the growth of our soul. It is only when we experience darkness in depth that we can really understand and embrace it.

Darkness, like light, is a source of energy. We thus cannot destroy it. Therefore, we must accept our darkness with love and compassion, in order to release, transform, and illuminate it. Resisting our darkness can cause fear and pain. We give more power to darkness whenever we resist it.

When we are angry with someone or feel angry about a certain event, this reaction actually comes from the dissatisfaction with ourselves that has been suppressed for a long time. Stimulated or triggered externally, such reactions manifest through our heart, because those negative emotions are eager to be acknowledged and released. When our heart is healed, we will discover that our worldview changes accordingly. Our heart determines the world we see.

When we can transcend our beliefs in duality and raise our level of consciousness, we will begin to understand that earthly life is an illusion. Every earthly experience is intended for us to learn about love and compassion. We must learn to love ourselves first in order to understand how to give love. Loving ourselves means giving ourselves permission to make mistakes without self-blame, and not negating ourselves or living with regret and guilt. Our earthly experiences are the lessons that we have selected pre-birth for ourselves. So, we should embrace these experiences and honor our choices, as they are the best we could do according to the level of our understanding and awareness at the time.

We must courageously confront all our negative emotions and endeavor to understand them. Our negative emotions exhibit our weakest areas that need much love, care, and nurture. They are also areas where healing and balance are required.

We can peel off our memories layer by layer and relive the events by facing the emotions, hurts, sadness, fear, helplessness, guilt, anger, etc., of our experience. They are the accumulated negative energies that our heart has suppressed and buried for a long time.

Release these negative energies through tears, and exhale, while telling yourselves,

"I am safe and protected. I am loved infinitely. Please discharge all negative energies from my cell memories and subconsciousness, as I have bravely completed my chosen experiences. I am grateful that my heart is balanced and healed, so is my body. I love myself the way I am. Everything is an experience. It is all an opportunity for learning and growth. All is well!"

With every release, our heart becomes softened and has more space for us to feel love. Love is always there. It is our negative emotions that shut down our heart and restrict our happiness.

True compassion begins with forgiving ourselves. We should no longer consider ourselves as victims. When we forgive ourselves, we can then learn to forgive others. Forgiveness of any experience is a powerful healing energy that can restore our heart to peace and harmony, while helping us return to our true self at the same time. Every time we forgive ourselves, we love and accept ourselves more. We also get nearer to our wholeness and resonate this beautiful essence with others.

True self is unconditional love. We are all beautiful individuals. We exist in eternal peace, joy, wholeness, and perfection. Our Heavenly Parents grant us unlimited love. Every one of us is beautiful and perfect to them. Because our Heavenly Parents are always with us, we can connect to their love whenever we face ourselves with honesty. Their love nurtures and heals us. As long as we ask, their love will guide us like a light tower and help us find our way home.

At last, I came to understand that the love of the spiritual world communicates with us through our "heart." Our heart is "home," is Heaven. We have never left "home." It is our separation-consciousness that hinders us from seeing the truth. When we accept every aspect of our expression as humans, and love ourselves unconditionally, we are returning to our true self. The purpose of all the external tools, including the books and articles we read and the lessons we learn, is to serve as guides for us to explore our own truth, to remember that we are love, and to cultivate our talents and power. We will then realize that we are "the one" we have been waiting for. Because we already have everything we need.

The Ascension of Mother Earth

I remember one morning in October 2015 when a very loud voice suddenly appeared in my mind: *Mother Earth, Unconditional Love!* I was shocked by this firm and powerful voice. I knew it was a message from the spiritual realm. I had been writing about our physical body at that time. It turned out that I was being guided to share the message of Mother Earth.

In recent years, symptoms of atopic dermatitis had begun to appear on a small area on my neck. I had thought that I was allergic to certain foods, and thus eliminated the suspects. However, in a short time, the rashes began to spread; first on my cheeks near my ears, then my hands, left lower leg, face, and on front of my neck. After experiencing dermatitis for a long time, I began to explore the messages my body was trying to convey. I eventually realized that these symptoms were a sign of my body's ascension. The negative energy stored in my cells was finally able to be freely released as rashes when I did not resist them.

Through the ascension of my body, I learned that our body is not our "true self." Our body is a sacred vehicle for our spirit to live in temporally. Our spirit has great respect and gratitude for the body because our body can provide the necessary life lessons and special experiences to assist our soulful growth and evolution. We cannot experience these things in the spiritual world. The earthly experiences, whether presented positively or negatively, are all precious to our soul. Our soul can accumulate many experiences and much wisdom through numerous reincarnations.

For centuries, people in Western civilization have regarded themselves and our Earth as a physical material form, separate from spirit, and most continue to view things this way. Scientists made a very important discovery in the twentieth century to change this perception—that ultimately everything is energy. Different vibrational frequencies and wavelengths constitute different forms of energy. Matter is a manifestation of a relatively slow vibrational frequency.

The Earth is a living body with consciousness and sensations. Like a loving mother, the Earth feeds all existence and nurtures us with abundant resources. The energy of the Earth gives us vitality and nourishes us through every cell of our body. It does everything to make us feel comfortable. It is our Mother Earth. She embraces us and loves us unconditionally. She supports us through our growth and heals us with her energy.

Most humans lack understanding, concern, and love for Mother Earth. Humans have done extensive damage to nature's ecological environment and its balance system. Many spiritually awakened people believe that the heavy energies contributed by our negative thoughts and emotions have accumulated to a point where Mother Earth can no longer sustain the balance of the environment. Mother Earth has initiated the necessary adjustments for self-healing through earthquakes, hurricanes, floods, tsunamis, forest fires, and so on. However, we need not be afraid of these disasters as they are not punishment. Their purpose is to bring the Earth back into equilibrium.

The life of humans and nature is closely interrelated; hence it is essential for us to coexist in harmony. We should care for the Earth with environmental awareness and not waste its resources. We should respect and thank everything on Earth because they are all sentient beings with sensations and feelings. They serve us with unconditional love to help fulfill our higher purpose.

We are going through the transformation process of planetary ascension. Mother Earth has created a higher dimensional parallel Earth with a new consciousness. The new Earth has risen to the fifth dimension and has entered a new position in the solar system. This 5-D Earth co-exists with the old 3-D Earth. We are thus living in a multi-dimensional Earth. These dimensions are not a place but a state of existence. The vibrational frequency generated by our state of consciousness determines whether our existence is in the third, fourth, or fifth dimensions.

Ascension is the evolution to a higher state of consciousness. All life on Earth is in the process of "ascension" and shall continue as such. Everyone has the free will to decide whether to ascend or not. The ascension of the Earth is important for the Universe. For that reason, the Earth has evoked full-scale assistance and support from the Universe. The Universe shall continue transmitting powerful light waves to help with the ascension of the Earth and all things on it. The energy of high frequency from the Universe can also bring great purging and purification. Our brothers and sisters of light are helping us transform and ascend as well.

Ascension starts from our heart. To invoke ascension, our heart, body, and mind are required to cooperate with each other. We need to break through the belief in duality on Earth (good/bad, right/wrong, etc.), let go of ego, and balance the karma. They are factors causing continued reincarnation and the separation-consciousness that needs to be integrated. Our body may experience symptoms such as headaches, joint pain, skin allergies, diarrhea, fatigue, etc. These ascension symptoms are due to the dense energy of our body, which cannot align with the energy of light. It is necessary to clean up the negative energy stored in the memory of the cells, so that the energy of light can flow through the cells of the body without hindrance, as cells long for love and light too. And our long-term suppression of inner fear and trauma will be re-experienced through our emotions, which will assist us in reexamining ourselves and finding answers.

We should fully accept this in-depth, transformational process of "self" by facing it bravely and telling it the following:

"Thank you for reminding me what I need to correct in my beliefs and thought patterns. Thank you for helping me release the unbalanced energy. You have completed your task and can leave now. I love you."

As the cleaning up continues to deepen, it will help heal ourselves and balance karma, taking us closer to the essence of our true self.

"Karma" is the cause-and-effect relationship produced by unbalanced energies between people. Karma is not a punishment or a debt. It is the unfinished lesson of growth, from this or a previous lifetime, which stores memories in the cells of the body and the subconscious. This unbalanced energy will appear in our life through repeated thoughts and behavioral patterns in order to help us find the core issues. Karma will use tests to aid us in the process of awakening.

Karma is dissolved when one or both people have learned to forgive. Forgiveness of any experience is a powerful healing energy. Forgiveness enables us to regain our life energy, as our energy is no longer attached to certain people or things. When we integrate with our soul energy, we can restore the balance and harmony in all aspects of our existence. We have then balanced our karma, and are no longer affected by personal, ancestral, or collective karma. We can then turn darkness into love and light.

Our thoughts are energy with creative power. Whenever we think, our thoughts will unite with similar thoughts to form a collective consciousness. Consequently, we should be careful what we choose to focus on. We must stay away from those events that could put us in negative emotions. These negative emotions can produce more conflicting energy for ourselves and the collective consciousness. When energy is in conflict, problems cannot be resolved.

The powerful energy generated from humanity's negative thoughts in the collective consciousness will continue to erode the subtle body of Mother Earth and cause her great pain. She will respond by using natural disasters to get rid of these energies and purify herself. We are all responsible for the state of the Earth. Changing the world starts with changing ourselves. Our thoughts, words, and actions are all made of energy. Every positive change we make for ourselves is the best way to help the Earth and the collective consciousness. As more of us become dedicated to improving ourselves, the collective energy will start to change. Together we can alleviate disasters and help Mother Earth move toward stability and harmony.

The New Earth is a planet full of light, unconditional love, balance, abundance, and joy. It is a state of Heaven on Earth. We have bravely chosen this special period to enter the Earth because our soul desires to bring light to the world.

We must love and respect Mother Earth as if it is our own mother. The love between Mother Earth and us has never been severed. She communicates with us through every one of our cells with her energy. I am very thankful to the Earth for providing our soul the school for learning and evolvement. I also appreciate the ascension of the Earth, which helps humans eliminate fear speedily in order to balance the karma from past lives and this life. We are jointly creating the new golden age on the Earth and participating in the process of human evolution. This is a great and joyful moment as we assist in the ascension of the Universe together.

I am grateful to the inspiration and guidance I have received from the spiritual realm. It not only opened up new horizons of knowledge for me, but also empowered me to understand our body, Mother Earth, and the ascension of the Earth.

12

My Life's Blueprint

*T*he blueprint I planned for my life is full of colorful and dramatic stories. I have gradually come to understand that my life's blueprint is a series of spiritual enlightenment and learning processes. All my earthly experiences have sparked my curiosity to know myself.

Aesina performed a spiritual enlightenment ceremony for me when we first began our work together in 2007. That was a very wonderful experience. It inspired me to know more about the spirit world and my mission with Aesina, who has been my mentor ever since. Whenever I have questions about the spirit world, Aesina answers them intuitively.

We have held our spiritual administrations regularly for over ten years. For the first several years, I was in a state of guilt over my past mistakes. I wondered if the Heavenly Parents would reprimand me. However, I could feel the Heavenly Parents' love in every spiritual administration. The energy of their love warmed my body and my heart. I felt that I was respected, understood, and accepted completely. I came to realize that with unconditional love there can be no punishment or judgment. What I had considered to be mistakes was because I was making judgments and coming from my fear. The profound purpose of our mistakes is to assist us in learning and growth.

Aesina would convey the Heavenly Parents' messages directly during our spiritual administrations. The Heavenly Parents would guide and inspire me according to the level of my understanding at the time. It enabled me to explore, comprehend, and learn from my life experiences. They never placed any demands upon me with a particular set standard but allowed me to be myself freely. They would reward me with encouragement and affirmation whenever I made even just a little progress. The Heavenly Parents' expression of love became the model and best example for me to learn from.

***

I recall the first time I met Jullian in 2007. I could not see him. Therefore, I would practice using my thoughts to communicate with him. Immediately after I sent out my thought, a surge of warm energy would fill the middle of my chest. As information is transported almost immediately, he had already come to my side. I learned that our thoughts hold energy; therefore, we cannot hide them. Thus, I began to pay close attention to my thoughts and learned to transform the energy of negative thoughts by recognizing and releasing them. Consequently, the busy thoughts in my mind are gradually quieting. We can live in the present moment more naturally when our mind is quiet.

***

On Ricky's thirtieth birthday in 2013, we were honored to invite Aesina to participate in this celebration. We held the spiritual administration in our home. Through Aesina, the Heavenly Parents had let me know about my life's blueprint and how I had planned my current earthly life in the spiritual realm. I had chosen, meticulously and wisely, my family members and friends. We had made soul agreements to offer each other valuable learning opportunities.

In order to realize the various plans for my life and fulfill my desired knowledge and experiences, I had found Ricky to help me. It was because he would give me lots of challenges as a mother. He would also help me learn how to love and communicate it with wisdom.

Ricky had chosen to experience drug addiction and severe depression in his life. Expelled from high school for the possession of drugs on school premises, he was sent to a juvenile detention house and juvenile probation camp. I was often worried about Ricky during that time, as well as filled with regret and remorse. I had trapped myself in a dark state of fear and anxiety.

As I began to comprehend my life's blueprint, I realized that we have planned everything for ourselves on Earth. My blueprint helped me to view my earthly experiences from the perspective of the spiritual realm. I understood that everyone is an independent individual. We have free will, which enables us to make choices and create our desired experiences. I had to learn the ultimate respect—respect for my pre-birth plans—to respect everyone else's choices.

This change helped me to accept and forgive myself, and the heavy latch on my heart was suddenly unlocked. Forgiveness granted my heart a feeling of relief and lightness. The tense atmosphere enveloping my home life thus melted away.

My husband spent a lot of time in our son's room after Ricky's farewell ceremony to sort out his belongings. Some items were set aside for donation; others were discarded. I admired him for facing Ricky's passing bravely, as every item contained a memory linked to his love for him. Taking care of Ricky's belongings stirred up many emotional fluctuations in my husband. I knew how hard it was for his heart to let go, how much he missed our son. There was a sense of helplessness in him; no longer would he have the chance to do the many things he had still wanted to do with our son.

So, we asked Aesina to help us communicate with Ricky. We were comforted by what we heard. Ricky gave us a precious gift: He is now at peace, filled with joy and contentment. Ricky could not have attained this state during his earthly journey. He also let us know that the true purpose of his earthly experiences was to prepare him to serve in the next life.

I finally understood the meaning and purpose of experiencing many dark sides of ourselves in life. It is to help us learn and grow through challenges and difficulties. These challenges also assist us in better understanding the thoughts and feelings of others so that we can help those searching for answers. All is designed for the expression of love.

***

In early October of 2016, I received a call from overseas informing me of the passing of my elderly father. Three days later, I requested that Aesina help me to communicate with my father during our spiritual administration. She stated: "Your father has already made his transition. He is communicating with us in the state of peace and joy. He is celebrating the completion of his mission and purpose on Earth. He is in Heaven where he feels truly at home. He has no more diseases nor any confusion. He is very free now. He has united with your mother like good old friends. They are excitedly reminiscing and sharing their earthly experiences."

I am thankful for this message from the spiritual realm. My parents were in fact good friends in the spirit world. They were willing to use pain and hurt to learn their desired lessons and serve the growth of their souls.

***

Once we are willing to transcend our dualistic way of thinking, and we no longer view the events of our life in terms of perpetrators and victims but can reflect on our life from a neutral stance, we will see the meaning and purpose in everything. The event itself is neutral, without the so-called right or wrong that we attach to it. Everything occurs in life for us to learn about love and compassion.

Our mistakes, physical illnesses, difficult trials, and negative emotions have all been arranged and planned before our birth. Therefore, we must appreciate our own courage and perseverance. They are the lessons we have desired to learn and the karma we wanted to balance.

We desire to continuously raise our consciousness and evolve spiritually. The free will we have is the sacred right of our soul. Therefore, we can create all the experiences we want in an infinite number of existences and expressions during our evolutionary journey. The Earth is a challenging school that provides us real-life learning experiences. In the dualistic nature of the earthly life, love can present itself both in perfection and imperfection. When we can find perfection in imperfect presentations and learn the wisdom in the process, we can expand our love and awareness and raise the level of our consciousness all at the same time.

We use a physical body only temporarily to conduct our life experience on Earth. Through spiritual awakening, we begin to realize that the separation consciousness of duality is an illusion. This is designed for the purpose of allowing us to learn and grow. We are a perfect whole. The unity of consciousness is our true reality. The only thing we can take with us when we leave Earth is our state of consciousness.

Observing the emotions and feelings in our heart with awareness will guide us home and return us to our true self. Our soul yearns to express its unconditional love in our life and bring light to the Earth. Every experience on Earth is meaningful and is what our soul wants. Everything is by the perfect arrangement of our soul.

We are One—a part of the whole and the source of life. All of life is divinely connected, and equally loved and respected. We all have support from the spiritual realm, including our higher self, and our spirit guides who we can ask for help at any time. When we are relaxed, open, and accepting, they will guide us through our intuition instead of our mind.

We are all beloved children of our Heavenly Parents and the Universe. We each serve in our own unique way. When we plan the blueprint for our earthly life, our incentive is love. I am so grateful to everyone for playing an important role to help others grow and evolve, and for helping one another to complete the mission of Oneness.

I am honored to be a spiritual "guinea pig," including but not limited to reexperiencing on Earth the process of the creation of the spirit. I am so grateful to the loving grace of the Heavenly Parents for creating every perfect brother and sister. They have never left us, as their love is always in our sacred hearts.

Every spiritual administration held through Aesina is full of love, joy, and inspiration. Its energy helps to cleanse and nourish my body, mind, and soul. And the messages of The Heavenly Parents continue to enhance my spiritual knowledge.

I deeply appreciate the unconditional loving support of Aesina, who helps me to walk on the right path in my spiritual growth. Besides serving as my translator, she has patiently organized the content of my writing and offered many helpful suggestions. I am truly grateful to our wonderful friend Ina for her years of kind support in many ways, including with this book, as well as to our editor Kendra for sharing her expertise. They are our spiritual team members.

***

I hope you will enjoy your unique self-discovery, as it is the journey to reclaim your true self. You need to look inward because this is the process for self-healing. You will begin to finally realize who and what you truly are. At the same time, you will remember your divinity, courage, freedom, wholeness, perfection, and infinity.

We are all dearly loved. All is perfect. All is well.

Made in the USA
Middletown, DE
28 December 2022

20624105R00121